Street Corner Theology

Street Corner Theology

Indigenous Reflections on the Reality of God
in the African American Experience

Carlyle Fielding Stewart III

James C. Winston

Publishing Company, Inc.

Trade Division of Winston-Derek Publishers Group, Inc.

TO SOW THE FALLOW SOIL

© 1996 by James C. Winston Publishing Company, Inc.
Trade Division of Winston-Derek Publishers Group, Inc.

First printing

PUBLISHED BY JAMES C. WINSTON PUBLISHING COMPANY, INC.
Nashville, Tennessee 37205

Library of Congress Catalog Card No: 94-60449
ISBN: 1-55523-687-1

Printed in the United States of America

To all the brothers and sisters
from the black neighborhoods of this land,
who live with dignity, have kept the faith,
and still trust in God

"Suffer, suffer,
suffer.
I ain't gonna
suffer
no
more."

—John Lee Hooker

Contents

Introduction

I have always wanted to write this book. It is the culmination of years of passionate involvement in black grass roots America, and it seeks to contribute positively to the field of theology.

The terms *street corner theology* and *indigenous African American cultural theology* describe the experiences that people have with God. The basic tenets of this theology have evolved not from the sacred canons of the university but from the mean streets of African-Americana. Street corner theology is not academic theology per se. It is not fashioned according to the basic presuppositions and formal hermeneutics of traditional theology but rather emerges primarily from the spiritual archives of African American cultural experiences.

Wolfhart Pannenberg developed a useful Christological typology that differentiates between understandings of Jesus from "above" or "below." For example, one might have a "high" or "low" Christology, either of which influences the nature and trajectory of theology. Jesus could therefore be analyzed as a man of history or the Christ of faith. In either case, one chooses the high or low ground in interpreting the man Jesus.

Similarly, street corner theology is from below for several different reasons. It is a theology whose principal archive is African American culture, which is the formative factor influencing all indigenous interpretations of God. This belowness differentiates life in the real world, the squalid hovels, and the back washes of urban and rural black communities from life seen through the eyes of traditional intellectuals and academicians in universities. Accordingly, street corner theology does not claim any specific cognitive traditions or intellectual predecessors.[1] It discloses reality on the other side of the railroad tracks, below the hallowed halls of academe. It is theology emerging from a world of music, laughter, babies crying, and people dying; a world of rappers, hipsters, funksters, and church-goers.

Furthermore, street corner theology, or indigenous African American cultural theology (I use these terms interchangeably), is theology whose primary sources are the down home, grass roots, folk elements and traditions which both shape and interpret the black experience in America. These traditions constitute the cultural archives from which all subsequent understanding of black life as a distinct cultural experience emerges.

The narratives of this text come from a wide variety of people, including a former gang leader, a homeless person, a street vendor, and other so-called social pariahs. The point here is to give voice to these unique people, all of whom have extraordinary stories to tell and have a philosophical and theological grounding that transcends their social condition. Their stories are theological inasmuch as they describe legitimate, real-life interpretations of God. These understandings of God are cogent, coherent, and tenable and could easily be placed alongside more formal theological discourse.

The ultimate concern here is for the spiritual vitality of African American people. Street corner theology is thus rooted in a culture of hope and filled with the positive expectations of the possibilities of God. Predicated on life in the streets or the church pew, the highways or by-ways of black life in America, the quest is for human wholeness, personal and spiritual transformation, and the establishment of authentic personhood.

The structural framework and theological method of street corner theology are presented in narrative form, which is closest to African and African American oral traditions. The narrative methodology of indigenous black theology thus posits the basic raw materials and preserves the simplicities of African American life and culture. In its primordial forms, the narrative more effectively reveals the peculiar textures and nuances of the African American experience. The oral transmission of knowledge and information emblematic of African American culture is best conveyed through the narrative form and is more closely aligned with authentic African folk traditions.

Moreover, the narrative form also preserves the dialogical elements of indigenous discourse, because there are myriad subtleties and peculiar inflections of meaning and feeling unique to black life and culture that resist full disclosure by abstract or analytical constructs. The story of one's "God encounter" allows the storyteller to speak of God in ways which preserve the structural integrity of the dialogical experience. What is experienced and felt about God is deeply rooted in the simplicities of black life. The who, what, and how of God are influenced by the contextual and cultural dispositions of black people. Ideas of God and their dissemination in the narrative form not only emerge from a cultural and a "lived" context, but they preserve the dynamic, spontaneous, and amorphous elements of indigenous thought. The context of lived experience in African American life and culture is thus transformed into the sacred text of theological construction.

So the primary sources of street corner and indigenous black theology are the lived realities and the cultural and spiritual archives of African American people. The sights, sounds, smells, and rhythms of black life are deeply rooted in the soul of African American culture, and what is sensed and felt about God is part of a continual revelatory process which can only be experienced by those shaped by the cultural and spiritual milieu of the African American experience.

Inherent in black life, then, is a level of sensed meaning, an experience of God which can only be profoundly encountered in the depths and breadths of black culture, in the fullness of its beatific embrace, or in the metered flirtations of its rhythmic pulsations. There is a passion, a texture, a quality of black life which makes it a vast oasis of cultural vitality. It is a reality that can only be known by people living within the thick, barbecue-basted, blues-jazz battered, Funk-Holy-Ghost-dipped experience of black life in America. Street corner theology, or indigenous African American cultural theology, is thus a grass roots cultural theology of African American people.

This book explores the lives of some extraordinary African Americans. The main data of this work has been garnered from thirteen years of full-time pastoral experience in the African American community. But more importantly, this book is based on forty-three years of living in the "hood," listening to the heartbeat and the soul of my people.

As a parish pastor, I gleaned valuable information that shapes the basic perspectives in this text. I have always known that grass roots African Americans have unique and profound understandings of God that the intellectual establishment seldom delineates or appreciates because they are so far removed from the everyday reality of black life in the streets. These stories of God are worth telling; they are of immense importance and value.

As a black man shaped by both the university and the streets, I value the education each has provided me. I have utilized that education to discover extant truths about how black people understand and create their own theology from an indigenous standpoint. The narratives that follow simply tell the story of God's existence and influence in the lives of these people. Their stories provide a deeper understanding of who God truly is for them, and they also create metaphors for who God might be for others in a larger context.

These experiences also involve a full complement of relational components and realities that create a hermeneutics which will both clarify and identify the unique character of black indigenous thought.

The following chapters include stories from individuals whom I believe represent archetypes of a variety of understandings of God from an indigenous perspective. I posed three basic questions in my encounters with each person. They are as follows:

- Who or what is God to you?
- How do you believe God is working most significantly in your life?
- What is the central or defining issue or experience in your life which has shaped your current understanding of God?

Each narrative is followed by a commentary which will help to clarify its general ideas. But before turning to these narratives, let us now examine the central tenets of street corner theology, or indigenous African American cultural theology.

---

[1]James Cone's Black Theology perhaps set the stage for indigenous African American cultural theology, but no specific intellectual tradition can claim it as a rightful heir.

The Foundation of Street Corner Theology

Long before the formal tenets of theology were developed in the academies and universities of this country, black indigenous peoples had developed understandings of God which emerged from the black cultural archives of lived personal experiences. The earliest theological formulations of slaves were shaped more by the realities of daily life than by the formalized dogmas of their white Christian masters. It was not until slavery had endured for several generations and slaves had adapted to the theological and cultural dispositions of their captors that Christian ideas of God began to take root in slave communities. But even then, as now, there has always been a remnant or subculture of black indigenous people who oppositionally developed their own theologies within and without the parameters of conventional Christian interpretation. Such a remnant has been translated today into a culture of the streets, where people creatively develop their own ways of seeing, interpreting, and interacting with the world around them.

The indigenous nature of these beliefs depends on the retention of those Africanisms, ideas, and presuppositions which were unequivocally oppositional to white, Western Christian interpretations. The indigenous perspectives fostered creative analysis and innovative modes of adaptation which helped slaves make sense of and endure their chaotic experience. This indigenous black theology was not influenced by the writings of other theologians or prelates of the church. It was not theology that evolved from professionally trained academicians. Instead, it was shaped in the continuum and realities of lived personal experiences. It was theology not legitimized by the sacred texts of white Western Christianity but sanctioned by the context of the African American cultural experience, rooted in the tumult, terror, agony, and ecstasy of black life in America.

Indigenous black cultural theology utilizes black culture as the primary context for theological reflection and is the foundation of street corner theology. Individual, personal experience is the primary datum of theology. It affirms and values subjective experience as a reasonable starting point for theology and asserts that lived personal experiences have more credence in shaping indigenous perspectives about God than anything else. This has been the case since slavery and continues to be true today in the urban frontiers of black life in America. There remains an indigenous remnant of believers whose sources and experiences of God are incongruous with orthodox theological suppositions. To them, God is a God of life in the streets whose purpose and meaning are both revealed and received within the complexities of the African American spiritual experience.

Indigenous black theology as the seed of street corner theology does not presuppose any previous paradigms of thought which claim to be wholly representative of the African American experience. It is theology rising from the vast corpus and culture of African American life and is therefore multifaceted and multidimensional. Indigenous black theology is not monolithic. While closely akin to the black theology of James H. Cone, it is not the final peremptory statement on black theology and black spirituality. It is simply one window, one avenue of the God encounter which has not been previously or thoroughly posited and explored by other theologians.

Indigenous black theology, while both personal and cosmic in scope, is equally concerned with the political, social, economic, material, and spiritual condition of African American people. Yet it is not political theology, and politics is not its guiding force. It is not theology that speaks exclusively to the social, political, or racial dilemmas of African American people but instead embraces the full spectrum of the African American spiritual and material condition. Indigenous black theology is concerned with the eradication of those political, material, social, personal, relational, and spiritual impediments preventing the full realization of human wholeness, the actualization of personal empowerment, and the spiritual and relational transformation of African American communities. It is concerned with the identification, exploration, and development of black spirituality and theology unique to indigenous African Americans. Its pragmatism lies in its capacity to raise African Americans' consciousness of their power and potential as persons of infinite worth. Indigenous black theology delineates the unique cognitive and spiritual orientation of African American people. Black ways of seeing, knowing, thinking, and being are shaped by both the black cultural archive and black spirituality.

Furthermore, African American cultural theology does not devalue the inherent worth of persons of other races, religions, or nationalities. While the elimination of white racism, sexism, and other "isms" impairing the realization of human potential and destroying people's sense of worth is essential, it does not denigrate the intrinsic worth of people as a means of forging a political agenda. It reveres the black self as the epitome of the sacred self for African American people; it is a self which should be nurtured, preserved, protected, and developed for the positive realization of human vitality and potential.

Indigenous black cultural theology affirms the healing properties of black spirituality and believes in restoring human wholeness and vitality to broken, oppressed, socially dislocated, and spiritually alienated people. Helping black people discover the reality of God as it relates to the ultimate concerns of their lives is a principal objective of indigenous black theology. Although these ultimate concerns vary, they have more to do with personal and relational empowerment through the realization of human potential than anything else. Indigenous black theology recognizes the relational and spiritual elements indispensable to human wholeness and embraces black spirituality as the foundation for all indigenous interpretations of God.

A further foundational assumption of indigenous black theology is rooted in the uniqueness of African American spirituality. This positive spirituality emanates from the indigenous African experience. It has created its own paradigm of human freedom and affirms that all life is created by God and is therefore sacred. The sanctity of life is not determined by individuals and societies. It is not necessitated by political or material forces in history. The sanctity of life in general and black life in particular is established through the realization of authentic personhood and culminates in the actualization of human potential. All life is beholden to the great spirit of God, which is the source and center of all things. African American spirituality is the foundation of indigenous black theology and is a formative factor shaping the archives of black culture which influence the formation of black consciousness.

African American spirituality, with all its profundity, tenacity, and dexterity, is the single most influential element shaping the character, trajectory, and structure of black indigenous thought. It is African American spirituality that constitutes the cohesive center, the solid foundation of indigenous African American faith and belief. It is this spirituality that differentiates black indigenous thought from all other indigenous interpretations and establishes the principal foundation of street corner theology.

The primary vehicle for understanding the intimacy and ultimacy of such sanctity is mediated in the actualization of human wholeness and the realization of personal worth and culminates in the harmonization of human relationships wherein people discover the value of self-worth through the realization of spiritual potential. The transcendent gifts of African American spirituality have encouraged African American people to surmount the social, political, and racial constraints confronting them and have congealed their infinite value as people. A transcendent, cosmic, and personal spirituality which maintains its own autonomy in the midst of volatile human conditions is a hallmark of indigenous black theology.

Furthermore, as stated earlier, the God of indigenous black theology is inclusive of, but not restricted to, the God of JudeoChristian traditions. Some aspects of indigenous black theology are not Christian and have not been primarily shaped by the African American church. It is true that indigenous black theology embraces the black church's influence on the formation of African American spirituality, but it also affirms a spirituality and knowledge of God which issues from the folk traditions and cultural archives of African-Americana. These understandings of God in indigenous black theology emanate from a variety of cultural sources, whose formative factors are shaped in the vast constellation of black experiences. These sources include but are not restricted to black religion and the black church, music, literature, art, black folklore and wisdom, humor, nature, science, and cosmology. Understandings of God emerge from life in the barroom, pool hall, the church, or the street corners of African American communities. Any assessments of the power, abilities, and magnitude of God's workings are derived from this vast lexicon of African American life and culture. Thus, this theology is indigenous in that it primarily emerges from the ideas, feelings, thought forms, ethos, and mythos of the African American cultural and spiritual experience.

If the indigenous black theological viewpoint has emerged primarily from the context of lived personal experiences of African American culture, then things such as jazz and guns, for example, have as much to do with developing indigenous theological perspectives as going to church, reading scripture, hitting the lottery, or eating health foods or rib tips.

Much of what is offered in these pages diverges from traditional theological interpretation. However, we cannot fathom indigenous black thought without considering the vast wealth of lived experiences shaping the peculiarities of black life and its subsequent interpretations of God. Accordingly, indigenous black theology contends that watershed, archetypal experiences within the African American cultural ethos serve as the organizing framework and definitive catalysis for shaping God-consciousness in African American indigenous theology.

The following narratives retain a purity, a simplicity unimpeded by the analytical constructs of traditional theology. God is experienced, and the narrator tells the story simply. As stated earlier, it is through the story and the metaphor that indigenous peoples best convey the meaning and interpretation of life around them. Black culture is the fertile soil from which the vital seeds of narrative discourse and their corresponding hermeneutical principles flower into full-blown theology. Street corner theology is an outgrowth, a by-product of the indigenous African American cultural experience. The cultural texts of African Americans emerge from the context of African American life.

The primary context, then, of street corner or indigenous black cultural theology is the African American experience. Black culture and black spirituality are the principal archives shaping all interpretations of God, and narration is the principal theological method.

The following narratives are designed to delineate a specific aspect of indigenous black theology. They are followed by commentaries expressed in more formal theological terms. By providing such analysis, we discover the inherent relevance and vitality of indigenous theology and the common ground it shares with conventional academic theology.

God of the AK47: The Sacred is the Profane

Hakeem Abdul Witherspoon, a twenty-five-year-old African American male, hails from the Bronx. His parents moved to Detroit when he was twelve years old. A former member of a Detroit street gang and now a student at a local trade school studying to be an electrician, he is full of nervous energy. He paces the floor like a caged and infuriated prisoner in solitary confinement, puffing heavily on a cigarette. With his head wrapped in a red bandanna, he is clad in black leather pants and a black motorcycle jacket with the words "Breeze Monkey" on the back. He pauses between puffs of O-ring smoke to speak his mind, and his words are charged with the rhythms and colors of black street culture as he flails his arms and hands like a symphony maestro. Dark horn-rimmed sunglasses shade his eyes as he urbanely speaks in cool, exaggerated measures. It is midnight.

Hakeem's Narrative

My first understanding of God being about magnum power was when fat Willie Day got three caps busted in his big fat behind by old man Rutherford while trying to squeeze out of his basement window. Willie Day, Fast Eddie McDowell, and myself hatched this lame-brain scheme of robbing Mr. Rutherford while he was away fishing. We'd been casing his house for three days and nights and thought he'd gone away on one of his monthly fishing trips. We had the whole thing planned, man. We could do no wrong. Except old man Rutherford came home early, just as fat Willie was about to attempt a bold escape. The whole thing was stupid. We didn't get nothing out of the house. What did Mr. Rutherford have, anyway? The whole thing was dumb from the get-go.

Anyway, old man Rutherford had just come home and heard this noise coming from the basement. He didn't know who it was. All he knowed was to get his .22 caliber. When he came rushing downstairs, all he could see was this big, wide, juju, jelly, pot-belly butt trying to squeeze through this too-tiny window. Big Willie couldn't go through the back door of the house like we did. That's the way we came in. He panicked and ran downstairs and was try-ing to get out of that small window when the old man came in. Me and fast Eddie had already gotten out—empty handed, mind you. But, naw, Willie had to fix a darned ham sandwich before he left. It was a shame, man. Seeing him get through that window was like trying to squeeze a ham hock through a needle hole.

Anyways, Mr. Rutherford shouted, "Halt, or I'll shoot!" Now, that was really some dumb stuff, because how was Willie going to halt? He was stuck in that window and couldn't go nowhere. Mr. Rutherford shouted again. "I said halt! Stop wiggling boy! What the hell you doing in my house? I got my kitchen magician, and I'm gonna fry me some hocks tonight!" Pow! Pow! Pow! Three blasts from his .22 caliber kitchen magician, right square into Willie Day's hind parts. Lucky it didn't kill him. But I think the old man wanted to teach him a lesson. He could have killed Willie dead in his tracks, but he didn't.

Willie was talking about pressing charges against the old man because of the mental anguish brought on him for getting shot in the behind. The whole neighborhood found out about it and teased

Willie for days. He was so embarrassed he didn't want to leave the hospital. He tried to talk his mother into sending him down to his grandparents in Mobile, but she wouldn't give him the Greyhound bus fare. He would have to take his medicine like a man. Everybody found out, and everybody joked about it forever.

We saw old man Rutherford some months later. He said he wanted to talk to us. We agreed to go by his house, mostly to apologize and thank him for not pressing charges for B and E-ing into his home.

Mr. Rutherford was a kind old dude, and I am ashamed when I think about how stupid we was. We had known him for years. He took us fishing once or twice. He was the type of cat who would give you his shirt. After his wife died, he seemed to reach out to us more. What we did was a crying shame.

He talked to us that day for a real long time. He talked about how growing up now was different than when he was raised in La Grange, Georgia. He said that the streets were dangerous and that we should be trying to get an education.

The old man never raised his voice. He always spoke very softly and slowly. He always took forever to say what he had to say. When old man Rutherford talked, we had better bring our lunch because we would be there forever. At the end of his talk he said, "True power in these times is respected only in fire power. You got a choice, fellas, the grave yard or the school yard. Take your pick."

Then he pulled out that stainless steel, pearl-handled .22. When he pulled it out we got scared as hell. Willie started sweating and shaking. "Now calm down, boys. Ain't nobody gonna hurt you. You see this, Willie?" he said, brandishing the shiny revolver. "Yes, sir," said Willie nervously. "This is the gun I shot you in your behind with. It's just a .22, but it's got the kick of a .38. If I didn't have this fire power, you all could have terrorized me and ain't no black man my age got no business being terrorized by nobody!

"So long as a man has fire power, he can protect himself and take care of what's his. Don't you ever think that power don't come this way. If you had known I was home and packing this .22, you wouldn't have thought about coming in here. This is power," he said, aiming the gun at the television set.

"But this here is nothing," he said, reaching into a black duffel bag. "I got a .45, a .44, a .38, a 30.06, and two double-barrel shotguns," he said, pulling the guns out one by one. "That's respect, baby. Smith and Wesson ain't got to earn no respect. Neither does Colt or Remington or none of 'em. When they talk, everybody listens.

"Don't be so stupid to not have something to back you up out here," he said solemnly. "You better get the biggest gun you can get to protect yourself," he said. We left after that, but I never forgot that conversation. The old man was serious. You'd better be packing your piece for protection and respect.

I decided that I would get the biggest gun I could get. Not a .22 or a .45 or a .44. None of that Dirty Harry crap. But an AK47 or a .357 Magnum.

My mind got made up real fast when my best friend, Victor Malone, got shot in the head at point blank range by two thugs sticking up a party store. He was an innocent bystander. We were standing outside the store eating potato chips when these two fools come out of the party store blasting. Victor died in my arms gulping his own blood. It was senseless, man. Like a whole lot of stuff that's happened since. Young black lives being snuffed out over nothing.

I made up my mind to get my own piece after old man Rutherford's talk and seeing Victor getting blown away like he did. The old man was right. In my neighborhood a gun gets you respect. You get even more respect when you're carrying your piece and everybody knows it. I went to get the biggest, baddest gun I could find. I wasn't copping it to kill nobody, but to protect myself from the young idiots and new jacks in the hood. I was tired of every Tom, Dick, and Harry running around showing off their pieces, talking about smoking somebody over the least little thing.

I thank God to this day for giving me the common sense to follow my first mind. Not too long after Victor got smoked, two young thugs cornered me on Vinewood and Grand River after a party at the high school. They just came out of nowhere. I could tell they had been drinking, because I could smell the booze.

They both rushed me. The one on the left was carrying a .44 mag with the long Clint Eastwood barrel. The other was packing a pearl-handled .45, Smith and Wesson. They rushed me with that hungry look in their eyes, talking about giving up the stuff. Back then, I didn't know what they were talking about, because I didn't drink, I didn't do drugs, and I didn't smoke. And I certainly wasn't selling no dope, not when every small-time dealer was getting smoked after only a few months of being in the business.

Anyways, they rushed me fast and hard, holding their "toys" up for me to see. "See what I got for Christmas?" said the tall one with the .44. "I'm Santa Claus, and I come not to give but to collect for Christmas! Give it up, nigga'," he said sarcastically. "Yeah, give it up!" shouted the other one nervously. "I ain't giving up nothing!" I shouted back, whipping out my sawed-off AK47. "I'm Santa's employer, Big Daddy, and there ain't going to be no Christmas this year or the next year or in the not-too-distant future if you chumps don't get out of my face."

I can't tell you the look in their eyes when they saw what I was packing. It's like they were frozen in time. Everything was slow motion. The tall one's eyes got big as silver dollars. The other's mouth fell down to his knees, and they both took off running. I can't tell you the sense of pride and power I felt defending myself in that way. I felt like Hank Aaron breaking Babe Ruth's record. I felt like Miami Vice and Prince of the City all rolled into one!

You see, where I come from a gun is about power and self-respect. It's about dignity and honor. This world is a dangerous and crazy place. When I hold my gun I feel strong. I know I can't get blown away just for nothing. I ain't going to be no fool. I ain't going to be gunned down on no corner. God would think I was a fool to let something like that happen.

See, I've thought about this. Most people don't see God the way I do. I've read all that stuff in church and listened to those jive preachers talk about Jesus. But had Jesus been packing his piece, Pilate and his boys and that other group of thugs and cutthroats wouldn't have jammed him like they did. If Peter, Paul, and Mary and the rest of that group had been carrying their stuff, poor Jesus wouldn't have gotten smoked like he did. All the time he hung on the cross, his partners still could have come back and wiped everybody out for doing what they did. The whole thing was wrong from the get-go. All this talk about sacrifice and shedding blood is Christian jive. That's fine, but that's why I ain't no Christian, because I don't believe in all that mess.

If Jesus had an AK47, there wouldn't have been no crucifixion. That's what's wrong with the world now. There's too many crucifixions, too many innocent people dying for no reason. It's all about self-respect and dignity. If God is God, he wants the highest and best for all of his people. If God is God, he's God of the AK47! God wants us to protect ourselves from all harm. God doesn't want people picking on others for no reason. The biggest gun stops stuff before it gets started.

Now, I'm not talking about using weapons to harm innocent people like a lot of these young punks in the street, or using them to smoke cops and other people trying to do their jobs. I'm talking about getting the biggest and baddest gun to protect myself from street thugs who want to smoke people for no reason.

God is about self-respect, honor, courage, and dignity. All that crap about sacrificing your life for the good of the whole at the hands of some maniac ain't what God wants for us. It ain't hardly self-respect. You preachers and religious leaders who talk that stuff should be ashamed. You're disarming the people. Once you disarm a man mentally and physically, you set him up for the kill. He's no good to nobody, including himself. Christianity disarms people and sets them up for the kill, just like with Jesus. And all for what? It doesn't change a single thing.

It's all about preservation and self-respect. If the Jews had AK47s, that crazy Adolf Hitler wouldn't have gotten so many of them to the gas chamber. Had they been packing in a real way, soon as the SS showed up, they would have been busting caps in everybody's behinds, and there wouldn't have been no holocaust.

The same is true for black people in America. When whites came to Africa, they had been worshipping the God of the new technology in Europe. They knew gunpowder and guns worked to enslave and conquer people. When they got to the shores of Africa with all them rifles and cannons and muskets, man, all we had was some jive bows and arrows, some outdated spears, and some stuff wrapped in pouches given to us by the medicine men to keep away demons. But them spears and them jive bows and arrows and spells from the medicine men were no match for them rifles and cannons. Guns and fire power changed the course of history. If we'd had more sophisticated weapons, we would have chased them white folks out of Africa, and there wouldn't have been no slave trade or no slavery.

Look at history, and you see that God is about power. Those who have the most powerful guns have beaten down their enemies. If God writes history, he has written it through the lives that were lost and the blood that was shed through the use of the gun. You can't deny that. God has written the history of mankind through bloodshed, and blood was always shed because somebody decided they weren't taking no more crap.

There is something in human nature that desires to protect itself, to stand up for itself. There is no other feeling like it, when you take a stand for the right thing. There is something in God that expects that from all of us. Do you think the drug dealers would be terrorizing our communities if the average citizen had an AK47? Do you think these young fools would be roaming and preying on people like they do? If everyone had an AK47, there would be real peace, because it would mean that these young fools would have to think twice about hurting somebody. Before smoking somebody, they'd think about being smoked, and that would cut out a lot of this craziness you see in the streets.

God ain't about taking no crap off nobody. When people talk that stuff about taking away the weapons, my question is if they take them away, who gets to keep theirs? What will the ones who keep theirs do to the ones who have to give theirs up? The problem is not the guns themselves but the fools who pull the triggers.

The AK47 is the gun of all guns. It's easy to carry. It has blazing speed, and it's deceptive. You can carry it concealed and nobody notices. There is no match for it on the streets. Sure, there are bigger and more powerful weapons, but none in the class of the AK47. It commands respect. It speaks softly and carries a big stick. When the AK47 speaks, even E.F. Hutton shuts his mouth. Remember that E.F. Hutton commercial? Just the mention of his name causes everybody to freeze. Everybody shuts up and pays attention. The AK47 commands more respect than that. When it talks, everybody listens. Everybody shuts up, and everybody has a long time to think about what life means to them. Every time people see it, they go into silent meditation and prayer. It's like being in church. Notice how people drop them heads and bow down when it's whipped out?

This gun commands respect. Those carrying it get respect. The technology used to make the weapon is top of the line, state of the art. Life is just a gun anyway. We all get shot out of the big Roscoe and travel like bullets through space 'til we hit our destination. When we hit our target, all life is stilled. Life is over then. God is the master creator of those things which allow us to shoot out of his big gun. We fly through life and then, like the bullet hitting its mark, we die. The same ideas God used to create life were used in the creation of the AK47.

Let me change gears on you for a minute, Reverend, and get deep. I can talk that stuff you preachers talk. You see, all life is sacred. The ground we walk on in our neighborhoods is sacred. The young boys in the hood are warriors protecting sacred ground and acting out their manhood. It's rites of passage. But the most sacred ground of all is the self, because God created the self as Holy ground. We have an obligation to protect this sacred ground.

God gave us this ground—our bodies, minds, spirits, and thoughts—and we must protect it by any means we can. All black people have is *themselves*. That's all we've ever had. The black self is a sacred self.

Malcolm had it right. We will defend ourselves by any means necessary. By protecting ourselves and arming ourselves, we are doing a sacred thing. It is an act of the holy. We are ensuring our own survival and preservation. It's an act of worship.

Out here in the streets, the sacred and profane, as you use it, run together. There is a thin line, and it's hard to tell which is which sometimes. When a man finds himself in the profanity of a real-life situation which threatens his life, he commits a sacred act by doing whatever is necessary to protect his life. Black neighborhoods are the stage where the drama of both realities gets played out with Hollywood flamboyance.

A lot of people think that what people do in black neighborhoods is bad, profane, unholy, unrighteous, but there is a level of the sacred which gets played out in unending blood rites and rituals, expressions of self-defense among the people. But when a man gets smoked innocently, that's the crime of all crimes, man. God really grieves then. God don't want people to die innocently in a senseless manner. Many drive-by shootings and deaths in black communities are sacred blood rites, where a man is protecting his sacred ground, which is himself. He is responding to a threat to his well-being. He is protecting the highest expression of life which God gives to human beings. His protecting his life is an act of praise and worship for that life. To not stand up for his life is to disgrace the sacred thing that God has given him and to disgrace God himself.

When I talk about the God of the AK47, I'm talking about that form of self expression which comes closest to God by protecting and preserving the self. The AK47 commands respect. It is the highest form of human preservation in the profanity of these mean streets. I have no problems when it's with me. I feel just as secure with my AK47 as believers do with their faith. Nothing else provides me with such confidence in these streets. When I'm packing my stuff, I feel like Jesus chasing the money changers out of the temple with his whip!

I feel safe, man. I feel free. I feel like king of the hill. Ain't no worries. No problems. No troubles. No concerns about somebody taking my life. To me, that's God, man. To have that kind of protection is truly having God at your side. God gives me that kind of security when I'm packing my stuff.

As long as I carry it, I have hope for another day. I don't worry about tomorrow because I know tomorrow will come. Without it, I'm open season, like a lamb before the slaughter. With it, I am protector of the sacred, preserver of the peace. God calls us to protect and preserve our lives through means which will prevent and correct a situation. My AK47 stops things before they get started, before things get out of hand.

I know what I'm saying, Rev, may sound vile, but I'm telling you my ideas about this whole thing. This thing of black life being sacred is real, man, and it ain't always about what you people in the church say it's about. God is much greater and bigger. God is doing all kinds of things that are different than what y'all been saying. And you know what I'm saying is true.

The greatest act of worship is not in senselessly laying down your life for others but in protecting the life God has given you in this asphalt jungle. It doesn't mean taking an innocent life or that innocent people should have to pay for somebody else's mistakes. I don't believe in all that.

God is a no nonsense God. He gives us common sense and the means to protect ourselves, our families, and our children. I keep thinking about how if we had more protection like this we wouldn't have had all them lynchings in the South of innocent black people. If more people had this attitude, we could keep a lot of unnecessary jive from our doorsteps. The Klan would have never been able to terrorize black people or anybody else. Because for every statement they made, we'd answer with a paragraph and an exclamation mark!

White folks wouldn't be bringing that crazy stuff around here unless they planned to pay up and pay up royally!

So everything boils down to issues of self-respect and the preservation of life. The innocent do not have to be slaughtered, because their lives are sacred. By having the AK47, you have the highest protection for yourself, and this is sacred.

I'm intelligent. I'm not stupid, Rev. I've had a lot of time to think about things and work out my personal theology, as you put it. I'm no fool. That's why I decided to make something out of my life by going back to school. I want to be an electrical engineer, but my real philosophy of life is the same. I still believe what I've just shared with you. Every person has a right to preserve and protect his or her life, and nobody has a right to take the life of another, except where his or her own life is being threatened.

Dignity, self-respect, courage, and honor. That's where God is, and that's what God is all about. We must do everything we can to worship and praise God. We can do this by protecting our lives the best way we can. The AK47 is the highest form of protection of the sacred life God has given us. It puts everything into perspective and gives the innocent an edge in these streets of no return.

Commentary

Many people would find Hakeem's interpretation of God atheological. Talk of guns, self defense, and God's mandate to protect the sacred black self diverges from conventional theological wisdom. Not gleaned from the sacred oracles of Christian literature, his theology is practically based on the laws of lived experience in the mean streets. These axioms value the sanctity of human life and affirm the right of each individual to protect himself against unwarranted harm by others. This is the highest form of human worship, protecting the sacred self from violation and annihilation.

The AK47 and .357 Magnum are metaphors for the individual's quest for personal power and self-respect in communities where both are easily trampled. It symbolizes the freedom of black people to protect themselves from all harm as well as to determine their own destiny. Hakeem's understanding of the AK47 is that it acts as a deterrent to those elements in the community that feast on the destruction of innocent life, because in African American communities, as with all neighborhoods, there are those who thrive on the shedding of innocent blood. The more vulnerable the innocent become, the more they become the sacrificial victims of these anarchistic elements. Thus, a kind of self-perpetuating blood-letting occurs wherein the lives of the innocent serve as the impetus for further terror and mayhem. A cycle of violence spins out of control, placing residents under siege with the absence of an effective deterrent. By carrying the AK47, Hakeem assumes sacred warrior status in protecting the sacred (himself), which is the first law of God. Such defense is compelled by a deep and abiding concern for the welfare of the innocent and the future of the community. Turning the other cheek to such nihilistic elements only fuels the rage of those determined to wreak chaos.

Perhaps most interesting is Hakeem's explication of the black self as the highest expression of the sacred in African American communities, that all black people should hold this self and themselves in highest esteem. For too long, African Americans have devalued themselves. They were taught to despise and reject themselves as people unworthy of God's goodness and mercy because of their skin color. The devaluation of the black self in particular and black life in general has been the central factor in the justification and perpetuation of racism and oppression in America.

Hakeem's interpretation reverses the debilitating affects of such beliefs. If all black people ultimately value themselves and the sacred life God has given them, they will do whatever is necessary to protect themselves from devaluation and destruction. This is the highest form of praise to God. The highest worship is to give thanks to God for life by protecting that life through any means.

For Hakeem, the Christian call to personal sacrifice at the hands of evil is a devaluation of the sacred. Christ's dying on the cross was therefore an abandonment of God's first law, protection of the sacred self. Christ's giving his life for us all did nothing to change the blood rites and sinful ways of humankind. Violence still mars the world, and communities remain paralyzed by fear. The willful, unwarranted sacrifice of human life is no act of the sacred but is instead by its very nature profane. Therefore, the protection of human life from the profanity of human annihilation becomes sacred.

To arm and protect oneself from the violence and evil of the world is a ritual of both practical and ceremonial value. Worship is that human activity designed to protect and vouchsafe the sanctity and value of human life. The sacred warrior and the true believers go about their acts of worship with the same values and zeal. The instruments of preparation are different in the church and streets, but the objectives are similar: acknowledgment of life's precious gift from the Creator and praise and invocation to the Creator for that gift through acts which simulate the rites of protection and petition to God through ritual acts of self-preservation.

The acquisition of the AK47 is illegal, and this is where the profane and sacred lose their clear lines of distinction. The fact that the AK47 is outlawed makes its appropriation for self-protection profane to some people. However, for Hakeem, the ultimate purpose in possessing it is the sacred preservation of human life, which displaces the larger cultural and religious moral condemnation. The profanity of illegal possession can never subvert the sanctity of personal survival, which prompts the ultimate valuation of life established through ritual acts of self-protection. If one must go outside of the law to establish law, order, and respect for the sacred status of people in the streets, then so be it.

Street corner theology does not repudiate the inviolability of certain laws, but it has never valued such codes as the ultimate guarantor of black self-preservation. From slavery to the present, blacks have not often been the beneficiaries of the American justice system but have instead lived outside its statutory protection. Living as outsiders has always had certain value for those blacks who never trusted in the American legal system for full protection. The fact that the AK47 is outlawed adds sanctity to the right of possession for some people. The issue here is self-determination. Possession of the AK47 becomes an act of the ultimate defense of the sacred, since it is a direct defiance of a system that cannot ultimately guarantee the sanctity and safety of black life. It is equally a deterrent to those forces and powers which have devalued black life through the continual shedding of innocent blood. Obtaining the AK47 is necessary, for no other weapon commands the respect, awe, and submission of potential adversaries. Protecting human life with weapons of equal value and power serves as no antidote to would-be assailants.

To both possess and use a weapon of this magnitude is sacred, since it opposes a system which can never ultimately value black life or guarantee the security of that life from all possible destruction. The point here is that black indigenous theology understands that the protection of black life is sacred, even if the means of protection do not fall within the parameters of the legal codes of society. Black indigenous theology does not repudiate the laws of society which are designed to protect human life. It simply does not revere those laws as the ultimate guarantor of human self-worth, value, or self-determination. Where legal codes fail to ensure the survival and security of the lives of black people, or any people for that matter, those individuals have the right to choose for themselves the means of protecting and preserving that life. The legal process cannot be the ultimate guarantor of the value of life.

Hakeem's value of life is not derived from Christianity or other world religions but has been honed through the canons of lived personal experience. Plain and simple. All life is sacred, and no one has a right to take the life of another, except in the protection of one's own life from harm. Even when the laws of society fail to protect its citizens (and this has been borne out by the historical record of America's treatment of African Americans), individuals can define for themselves the appropriate means of protecting the sacred life which God has given them. The means of defining what is sacred can never be wholly trusted to the larger society, especially since that society has devalued the sanctity of black life in the first place.

Hakeem's theology in its indigenous form affirms that human life is sacred and that protection of that life through the best means available is an act of worship. The AK47 is a metaphor for understanding the complexities of the human struggle for dignity, honor, and courage amid adversarial and devaluational social realities. It typifies the human quest for spiritual and practical self-determination amid some realities which cannot confer ultimate value through laws, ethical codes, and political order.

Street corner theology does not endorse the acquisition of outlawed weapons for self-defense. This narrative simply provides a glimpse into the logic and rationality of a theology of the streets which posits a legitimate viewpoint. The Hakeems of the world have a "sacred warrior" mentality which develops its own moral codes based on the laws of street life. The sanctity and worth of those codes are held in the highest esteem and are believed to empower individuals in their quest for peace, freedom, and human tranquility, notwithstanding the disabilities of the larger culture and society.

Lord of the Digital

His name is Larry Hotchkiss. He's a forty-two-year-old gay male dying of AIDS in Harper Hospital, and he's lying in his bed in the fetal position. He is a former taxi driver who was once a robust 205 pounds, but now his frail, emaciated 115-pound frame is punctured by IVs, tubes, and other life support systems. His countenance exudes the same terror and pathos of a starving victim of the Jewish Holocaust. A solitary tear gathers in the corner of his left eye, and his speech is labored like that of a winded boxer after twelve rounds of hard fighting. Digital monitors crowd the room, and he studies them with a Kevorkian-like intensity. A compact disc recording of Billie Holiday's "My Man" plays softly from a dimly lit corner of his room. It is midnight.

Larry's Narrative

Now that all the people have gone, I have a lot of time to myself, Reverend, to just think about my life. They say when you're about to die, your whole life flashes before you. But because I'm dying in this slow, painful way, it seems that my life history is moving in slow motion.

I told the hospital staff not to allow my lover, Harold, to come here anymore. I know that broke him up, but I just couldn't stand him coming here and crying all the time. It's depressing enough to handle this disease without all that crying and carrying on. Do you think I was wrong for telling him not to come? Oh, well, what's done is done. I do miss him sometimes, though.

My family is the same way. They come here and "boo hoo" the whole time. My father never accepted me when I came out. He disowned me and said I was not his son. He's been here a few times, but he made me feel so uncomfortable because he never knew what to say. I wanted to spare him the aggravation of coming here, so I told him not to come anymore.

People say I shouldn't deny my family the opportunity to see me, but if their seeing me only makes me feel more depressed, why should I?

I've been thinking about God a lot lately. I've been working out my theology. Rev, you're always telling us to develop our theology, and I've had a lot of time to think about God, what God means to me, how I've lived my life, and where I'll go when I die. Between doses of medicine and the conversation from these machines, I can tell you a lot about God I never thought about before.

There are three things of which I am thoroughly convinced: that God is the master of pain, the author of authentic personal truth, and the granter of personal serenity and peace.

Since contracting AIDS, I have learned to live with pain. I know that God is the master of pain, that the closer we truly move to God, the more we can master pain. There have been some days when the pain was so great that I couldn't even scream. But praying and talking with God has helped me tremendously. The more I pray and talk with God, the more the pain seems to go away. God is definitely related to our pain. God is my anesthetic.

One day it dawned on me that Jesus' crucifixion was a lesson in the mastery of physical pain. Jesus' whole life was about imparting ways for us to master the spiritual, emotional, psychological, and physical pain in our lives. The conquest of the pain of the crucifixion is exemplified by the resurrection. God specializes in mastering the pain and suffering of our lives. The closer we move to God, the better we develop the techniques for the re-sublimation of pain's devastating effects on us.

Why is there so much trouble in the world? If you look closely enough, you'll see the issue of pain somewhere in the mix. Why do these young kids act out their violence? Because of the pain of some past experience. Somewhere along their path they were hurt deeply by someone and couldn't master the pain of that encounter. So they act like a fool and cut the nut on somebody else in frustration.

I tell you, I've had times when the medication wouldn't take away the pain, but focusing on God and calling on his name did bring relief. God is a pain master. If we listen closely to what God is saying to us, we'll hear him tell us how we can get on with our lives despite our pain. If we listen closely, we can truly hear. I hear God speak all the time, mostly through the beeps of these digital machines. God speaks directly and clearly through them. Challenges to overcome the pain always come from him.

When I told my parents that I was gay, I braced myself for the pain I would cause them, but I still knew that it was something I couldn't help. I hurt a lot of people when I came out of the closet, but I hurt myself more by staying in. I knew I was gay—well, let me say I knew I was *different* when I was three years old. I didn't like to do the things boys usually do. While they played baseball, I stayed at home and secretly played with my sister's dolls. Everything was a secret. I tried to keep things in, but it caused me more pain because I was living a lie. I lived to please everybody else but myself, so when I decided to come out of the closet, I had made up my mind that I wasn't living with the pain anymore. Coming out helped me to master the pain of my life, because I wasn't happy. The personal truth of my real identity compelled me to come out. God is a God of truth, and I had to own up to my true identity and feelings.

I knew that God wasn't happy with me. Not because I was gay—I believe God created me this way—but because I wasn't being true to who I really am. I know the Bible condemns homosexuality as sin, but I believe my living the heterosexual lie did more to displease God than the fact that I was homosexual. This may sound like a cop out, but it's true. If God helps us to master the pain of our lives, then I know that God helped me to come out of the closet. Coming out was a liberation of my mind and soul. It was a way for me to deal with the pain of my life situation. Once I came out, the pain of living the lie subsided, and I was able to get on with my life. God always wants us to face the personal truth of our lives. However painful that truth is, God gives us the power and spirituality to face it. What is spirituality, anyway? It's equipping people to deal with and overcome the affects of truth. That's truth with both a big and little *t*. It's the ability to come to terms with the truths of one's life with God's help. It's facing oneself nakedly, squarely, and without the benefit of avoidance rationalizations.

Coming to God is coming to truth. How can I say God is truly in me when I'm afraid to face the truth of my homosexuality? Facing and telling the truth about that was like letting the God locked up in me for so many years go free. When I faced and confessed my personal truth, the God in me was set free!

And now that I am dying of AIDS, I do not regret being homosexual. I am what I am! I am sorry it has come to this. I am sorry for the pain I have caused others, but my being HIV positive does not dissuade me from believing that I did the right thing.

Before I came out, I went to counseling and therapy and got all kinds of professional assistance. I wanted to see if there was a clinical problem. Perhaps there was some congenital defect that could be corrected through clinical intervention. But after all this, I was convinced that being gay had nothing to do with a clinical problem. I'm just that way. Plain and simple! I think I caused God more pain staying in the closet than coming out. I truly believe that many gay people are congenitally predisposed to becoming gay. I have always been this way. God created me this way. It's not something I learned socially. I am God's definition of the new humanity. God created something new in gay people.

Now, as I lay dying, the numbers on the digital readouts on these machines and that clock on my nightstand are my only consolation. Every day I watch the numbers. Every day I study the readouts. The numbers on the digital displays tell it all. When I lay alone in my room, the glow of the red numbers provide a solace that only the lonely and dying can know. I know this technology with the digital readouts has a power, an authority that cannot be superseded. They speak for God in a sense. Yes, they are artificially made and electronically controlled, but these digital readouts tell it all—whether I'll live or die, what state or condition my body is in. The numbers have a great power for me. They are monitors of my soul. Everything from blood level to heart beats, these machines scrutinize me daily.

If I wake up in the morning and the numbers aren't too promising, I try to rally my body so the readouts will change in my favor. You know, it really is a thing of will. Sometimes I feel I can will those numbers to come in with a better score. Some days I'm batting a thousand. Other days I'm way below average.

The God I know and talk to these days is not only the master of pain but also the Lord of the Digital. The technology given to us today reflects the mind of God as much as it does the mind of man. Without those numbers, I am nothing. I am a non-entity. Each day I look forward to the digital readouts. They tell me so much about what God is doing and will do to sustain me or take me. The digital is the mind of God pronouncing judgment on my living each day. Each breath I take and each pulse I have comments on the condition of my body.

Some days I know when the numbers will not be favorable, and I get depressed. But seeing those numbers gives me strength also. There are days when literally all I can do is lie and stare at the numbers on the digital machines. There are no voices of consolation or comfort, no cheers or accolades. There are only the sounds of the digital machines moving from one number to another, building a museum, a sanctuary of thought for me. Concentrating on the numbers allows me to transcend time and space. I can look at the numbers and literally concentrate myself away from my room and the people around me. The digital monitors have helped me perfect my powers of concentration and meditation, where pain is obliterated and anxiety ceases. By focusing on the numbers, I free myself from all bodily and spiritual restraints.

I watch the clock a lot, too. I am fascinated with time. Why? I guess because I know that I don't have much time left. There's something about the way those numbers on the clock flash from one digit to the next, something which speaks about the nature of life itself. One minute here! The next minute gone! The digital clock flashes swiftly, after a long pause on a minute. Then swoop!— the number changes. My life seems to pause on the minute. I am suspended there between life and death, and just like the digital clock which quickly flips from one number to the next, I hope the Lord takes me just like that. I don't want to be held in suspended animation. Just take me Lord, like the flash of the numbers on this digital clock!

In the old days, time was measured on clocks which had faces that you could see. Now the digital clocks give a different readout of time. You don't see the entire face of the clock, just the quick flash of numbers, minute by minute. There are no second hands, just the numbers on the digital display. Perhaps our lifestyle and understanding of time is related to the flash of numbers. Swift, exacting, and final.

It seems that my life hangs on the flips of the numbers. Minute by minute I am held between life and death. So long as the numbers on the digital readout don't change, the verdict is life. I have reprieve. But once they flash, I know my time is short. God is Lord of the Digital. It is he who holds the power of time and he who sustains our lives between the quick flashes of death and life's uncertainties.

These machines and their readouts have given me nothing but hope. Each day that I have an opportunity to read the numbers is a blessing from God. I have studied these machines. I know this technology. The digital is truly a source of affirmation and confirmation for me. But I know there will be a time when the numbers will not turn in my favor. Each flip of the clock will be a countdown to eternity. On that last turn of the clock, I hope I'm ready to make my heavenly ascent. God is the master of pain and Lord of the Digital. It is he who controls it all and pronounces the final judgment. I just thank God that I've had a chance to live and have these few precious moments of life. It's all about the digital readout. This is the most important thing to me now—the red numbers on those big black machines!

Commentary

Larry's idea of God exemplifies a capacity to transcend personal pain and suffering. Although he is dying of AIDS, the disease and its ravages are not the linchpins of his understanding of God or his sense of personal identity. It's interesting that the life-support machines and the technology used to sustain his life, rather than the pain he felt from affects of the disease, became the focus of his theology. If God is the master of pain, then God would help Larry to overcome his pain as he moved closer to death. If God is the author of personal truth which leads to authentic existence, then God would sanction Larry's disclosure of his homosexuality, since living in the closet was the penultimate expression of truth.

Larry's theology correlates the notion of Lord of the Digital with God as the author and controller of all time. Digital technology becomes a metaphor for interpreting how God enables him to deal with personal suffering and develop his powers of spiritual concentration. While the machines are created by man, God is still the omnipotent source whose mind propels the machine's vital functions. The purpose of the technology is not to save life but to sustain life meaningfully amid death's imminence. The machines provide their own form of meditation, their own litany of relief. For Larry, the digital life-support mechanisms are not only life-sustaining but life-affirming. With the breakdown of vital and supportive human relationships—his family and friends no longer came to see him, partly by his own choosing—came the objectification of digital technology as a source and foundation for personal vitality and meaning. When people could no longer provide comfort to him in his terminal condition, he looked to the life-support technology as a means of sustaining hope. The digital would give a meaning to his daily struggle for life that people could no longer provide.

The critical notion here concerns a theology of transcendence (which is a hallmark of indigenous black theology) and the objectification of consciousness based on relationships with objects that provide meaning and recourse to the purposelessness and absurdity of human circumstances. A central component of indigenous black theology is the ability of believers to transcend their particular condition while remaining optimistic and hopeful that God ultimately gives meaning to their lives. The challenges presented by personal pain, suffering, and social alienation never supplant God's capacity to help people find personal meaning, self-worth, and authentic existence. A way to overcome the meaninglessness of object-status resulting from social ostracism is to develop a relationship with the object which transcends all the prescribed categories of conventional meaning and interpretation.

Larry understood that homosexuality was sinful according to the scripture, but the biblical condemnation of his actions did not thwart his sense of worth and personal meaning as someone who believes in God. The biblical-Pauline mandates against homosexuality did not prevent the establishment of his meaningful relationship with God, nor did they stymie his development of a positive self-concept as a worthy recipient of God's love. Where the social and religious powers provide no perceived avenues of personal meaning, the individual creates his own sanctuary for the discovery of self-worth. This may mean the establishment of vital connections with those objects ordinarily conceived as idolatrous by normative religious interpretations.

Larry struggled to come out and firmly believed that his disclosure was more ethically pleasing to God than living his sin in secret. Homosexuality notwithstanding, his quest was for wholeness and vitality, the realization of human potential which could only result from revealing his true nature and being. The centrality of personal truth in the quest for authentic being and existence despite social and biblical denunciation is an important aspect of his personal theology.

Again, indigenous black theology affirms that the sanctity and value of the human person is more important than the sin of personal lifestyle choices. Larry's spiritual worth as a person of God supersedes his social identification as a homosexual person. Indigenous theology is not *ad hominem* theology, wherein the worth of individuals is devalued because of life changes and choices.

Larry's understanding of his spiritual worth as a person was not subverted or defined by his social condemnation. His merit as a human being extends beyond such categories and considerations because they exceed the moral valuations and judgments of conventional religious evaluations and transcend the devaluations which come with being labeled homosexual.

In other words, while recognizing his own lifestyle as being sinful according to biblical precepts, that judgment did not preclude his quest for human wholeness, personal fulfillment, and a meaningful relationship with God. Indigenous black theology recognizes the importance of scripture from various religious traditions but does not interpret that scripture as having final, peremptory judgment about the sanctity and inherent worth of people. The fact that scripture condemns homosexuality as sin does not prevent the homosexual person from finding purpose, value, and meaning in a lived revelatory context.

The point here is that long before and after the belief in the sanctity and authority of scripture was established through the Christian faith and church, black people have found meaning, purpose, and worth as people. They believed in their value and worth as creations of God long before the advent of Christianity. This is indigenous truth. Even today, numerous black people who have not inculcated scriptural truths and are not members of particular faith communities have developed meaningful personal theologies not wholly conditioned by Christian presuppositions and precepts. This hallmark of indigenous black theology, while affirming the importance of Christian scripture, does not confirm any sacred writings as the final peremptory pronouncements on the ultimate worth of people. This does not mean that homosexuality or other sins cannot be legitimately judged by the standards and precepts of established religious faith. It only means that the ultimate sanctity, worth, and value of people cannot be finally determined by the axioms of scriptural texts but must issue from the lived truths of personal experience. That ultimate value can only be derived from personal experience with God.

These individuals have always exceeded the established parameters of faith and have somehow managed to develop a relationship with a living God which transcends all processes devaluing the sanctity of black life and worth. The context of personal experience is far more valuable in developing personal meaning than the precepts and prescripts of previously determined ethical codes.

Indigenous black theology has always helped black people to overcome the perils of human devaluation and depredation resulting from racism and other social condemnations. Inherent in indigenous black theology is the idea that the human person and his or her value in God's eyes are ultimately more important than the social, racial, or sexual classifications used to reduce and define his or her sense of self-worth. Labels may be used to describe a condition of the person, but they never define the person's self-worth in the eyes of God.

Objectification of meaning with that which has already been objectified and transcendence beyond the established codes of scripture as the revelatory context for the discovery of personal meaning and value are hallmarks of indigenous black theology.

Larry died three months after our last interview. The fact that he contracted AIDS as a result of his homosexual lifestyle did not diminish his claim to authentic personhood. He stated in his last days that if he were to live his life over again, he would still be true to what God had created him to be. He had claimed his truth and had lived it notwithstanding the consequences. Larry died with his eyes open, facing the digital life-support machines which had sustained him through the pain and suffering brought on by this devastating disease.

God of the
—How I Got Over—

Her name is Julia Weathersby. She is thirty-five years old, unmarried with four children, and she sells hot dogs on the streets of Chicago. The deep lines in her dark brown face and the thatches of gray hair on her temples are those of a woman much older than she. Her swollen hands and the bags under her eyes tell the story of her physical abuse, and her pupils shadow thin mists of glazed sadness in eyes sparkling with glints of betrayal. She speaks in soft, warm tones. The southern turns of her measured phrases display a Mississippi brogue. Her voice chirps like the melodies of migrant birds in spring. There is something enchanting in her words as her voice breaks, and her sentences are punctuated by long, thoughtful silences. She is guarded and cautious as she tells her story. It is twilight.

Julia's Narrative

I knew something was wrong when my mother up and left in the middle of the night. I'll never forget that night. It was cold—thundering and lightning. Felt like the roof was coming off the house. Mama and Daddy had a terrible argument. They was always arguing about something. They was always fighting. Tension stayed in our house, like all hell was breaking loose, like evil had come to stay there forever. We never was happy as kids 'cause my parents were always at each other's throats.

The roughest fights would always end up with Mama screaming at Daddy at the top of her lungs. She kept screaming about him messing with the two oldest girls, Lila and Mary. I'm the third oldest girl in a family of seven children. My two oldest sisters are five and six years older than me. But Mama would always be screaming at Daddy about messing with the girls, and I never could figure out what she was talking about until two years after Mama left and Lila and Mary had been gone about a year. The girls didn't stay long after Mama left. Guess they couldn't take it no more. They had had enough.

Mama stormed out that night. All Daddy said was, "Take your black behind on, then, and don't never come back here no more!" He was mad, but it didn't seem like he cared whether Mama stayed or left. He seemed like he didn't care one way or the other.

All the time they would argue, I could remember having long talks with God, asking him to make them stop their fussing and carrying on. I remember always finishing my talks with God and asking the same thing. "Are you there, Lord? Where are you, Lord? We need you, Lord! Please come by here and bring peace to this house, Lord!"

Anyway, times got worse. When Mama, Lila, and Mary left, the weight of raising my four younger sisters and brothers fell mainly on me. I was working a job at a local store, going to school, and trying to serve as a mother to my younger brothers and sisters.

When I think about it, I was too young and too busy to be angry at my mother for walking out on us. But I still had my long talks with God into the wee hours of the night, and I would always ask, "Are you there, Lord? Where are you, Lord? Please give us the strength to go on, Lord!"

Sometimes it seemed that God would answer, because right after my prayers things between Mama and Daddy would calm down. It was as almost as if God said, "I have heard Julia's prayers. Now I want you all to stop all that fussing and cussing and act like human beings." Right after my prayers, Mama and Daddy would be all hugged up. Things would go well for a few days, but then we'd be right back in a mess. But I know God was speaking to my parents because of my prayers. They just decided they would ignore what God was telling them.

My family never was too religious. We never went to church. Daddy always said that the church was full of hypocrites and that preachers wasn't nothing but pimps. I have been in a church once in my whole life. Although they never went to church, Daddy would say prayers before meals, and I could always hear Mama praying at night. And even though I never went to church, I always believed there was a God. I always had faith that God would somehow take care of his children. But I've always wondered if God was really there. Sometimes things would be so bad, it just seemed that God was nowhere around. Like he lost control of the universe or put an "out to lunch" sign on the door because we humans were raising too much hell for him to deal with.

As I said, things were getting touchy, and then all hell really broke loose. I knew there would be some problems, because not too long after Mama, Lila, and Mary left, I noticed my Daddy looking at me a certain way. I couldn't really explain it, but if I was bending over cleaning something in the house, I would catch him looking at me in that strange way that a man does when he wants a woman. He would be acting real funny, almost like he was the devil himself.

I was afraid of my father because he struck me with a fear of holy hell. It was like he had this evil hold on my life. I remember once when I was washing dishes he came by and swatted me on the behind. Now, I thought to myself, what's his problem? Why would my own father touch me on the behind like that? I couldn't say nothing, so I went in my room, laid down on the bed, and cried like a baby.

Little things like this began to happen more and more. Daddy would be real fresh with me, and I remember my little brother Willie asking one day why Daddy was doing those things. But that wasn't the killer.

One night when I was in my bed, I felt the presence of this body laying gently down beside me. I was thinking to myself, "Could I be dreaming? Who could be getting in the bed with me? Is it Willie, David, Sharon, or Grace?" I knew it wasn't any of the younger children because the force of the body on the bed told me it was a grown body, a powerful body. It was a body that was funky and smelly. It was my Daddy's body.

I was so scared I began to shake. All of a sudden I felt this hand reaching over and touching my breasts, and I heard those terrible, dreamlike words. "You know I love you, baby? You know I love you?" His hand began moving up and down the front of my body. My back was turned to him, so I couldn't see his face. The room was pitch black. Then he put his hand in my vagina and made this dog-like moan that scared me to death. I was paralyzed, frozen in time. I couldn't move. His hands moved faster and faster over my breasts, stomach, and vagina as he murmured senseless words about loving me and needing me and wanting me. My heart cried out. My soul screamed in agony, "Are You there, Lord? Lord, God, where are you? Please don't let him rape me, Lord! Lord, show your face or something! Please help me, Lord!"

All I remember is that I passed out. It was like my spirit left my body in one hell-fire moment. My soul was screaming for God, but I couldn't say a word.

When I woke up, my night gown was damp with semen. My vagina was sore. There was blood on the sheets. I was seventeen and a virgin. My father had taken my virginity. I was a nervous wreck for weeks after that. I cried for days on end. And Daddy acted like nothing ever happened. "What the hell's wrong with you, Girl?" he shouted. "Stop all that darned crying and make me some dinner."

Things were never the same after that. About three weeks later he came to my room again. After the first episode, I kept my room locked at night. I never could sleep after that. But he just burst the door down and got in the bed. For spells he would come to my room every night. Sometimes he would take me. Other times he would just fall asleep with his hands on my breasts, snoring loudly. It was horrible. I wanted to kill him. I wanted to tell somebody what he was doing to me. But I could only talk to God. It was my talks with God that kept me together.

I remember falling into a deep sleep one night after one of my long talks with God. I could see and hear God so clearly. I could see him with the look of dismay on his face. He said, "Now, Julia, I don't want this to happen to you anymore. You've got to do something about this situation. Your father is a very sick person, and you must do something to get out of there or get him some help." I remember every word God said to me that night. I'll never forget it.

The problem got worse when I found out I was pregnant with Timothy. I was pregnant with my father's child! I told him one night and he just looked at me with that evil stare and told me to go see Mrs. Mullins so she could fix the problem for me.

I felt like a prisoner, like I'd been given a life sentence. Death row would have been better than what I was experiencing. I felt ashamed and violated. I never felt God had left me all alone, though. I knew God would help me through this, but there were times when I would just ask over and over, "Are you there, Lord? Are you there?"

I refused to kill the baby, I think because I had become sick myself. I wanted to keep the baby as a terrible reminder of how he had violated me. It was a bad decision.

After Timothy was born, Daddy accused me of sleeping around with the boy next door, Terry. He kept calling me "whore" and "slut" and said that bringing someone else's baby into his house was a disgrace to him and his family. It was like he had no memory of what he had done to me, that Timothy wasn't Terry's baby, but his baby!

My father put the rumor out in the neighborhood that the baby was Terry's. He began running Terry down in front of other people. One day Terry confronted me. "What's this I hear about your father saying I made your baby? What's wrong with your old man? Has he lost his mind? I don't appreciate him dogging me like that! He's got everybody thinking it's my baby, and you and I are just friends. Your old man is really sick. He's got the whole town thinking I fathered that big-head boy of yours. The kid look like he's his, anyway."

After years of incestuous abuse I knew it was time to go. The violations did not stop even after Timothy was born. I knew that something would have to be done before I killed him, or killed myself. Things had gotten that bad. Everyone in town was even saying the baby was my father's.

This was the most difficult time of my life. Hard trials, hard trials. There was no one I could talk to during those days but God, and I know that God brought me through this.

I was too ashamed to have friends. I felt the whole town of Magnolia knew that my own Daddy had fathered my baby. It seemed that when I went to work and to places in town, people stared at me with that look of hatred. People just looked at me like I had lost my mind. No one ever said much to me during that time. I would come home from work and lie across my bed and cry like a baby. It seemed no one really cared. But I always had a friend in God. I knew that God would answer my prayers. But I would always ask, "Are you there, Lord? Can I get over this?"

I had a lot of anger during that time. I was angry at myself for letting this happen, for not killing my father, and for allowing him to violate me. I was angry at other people because I could turn to no one to talk about my problem. I was angry with my mother for walking out and leaving us cold. In fact, we never heard from her again. I don't know to this day if she's alive or dead. But most of all, I was angry with my father for raping me and keeping me prisoner as long as he did. Really, anger is not a good word describing how

I felt about him. It was more like hatred. I knew my father was sick, but that didn't matter to me. It still didn't stop the agony and pain I felt for what he did.

But I still kept having my talks with God. And then I had another dream. This time God told me that I had better get the hell out of there, that I should pack my bags and leave on the first thing smoking out of town. But I felt guilty. I was torn up inside because I just didn't want to up and leave my younger brothers and sisters, and it was still a home for Timothy. I could see God's sweaty, black face in my dream yelling, "Get out of there! Get out of there! Get the hell out of there! Nobody has a right to do to you what your Daddy is doing to you. Get out of there, Julia! Save yourself." God had been saying this for a long time. Long before Mama left, but I refused to listen to him.

I couldn't leave, and the dreams never went away. They kept getting stronger and stronger, with God's voice getting louder and louder, until one dream I could see him screaming at me. I could see blood coming out of his mouth and tears in his eyes. I saw his wrists were slashed and blood was everywhere. He was swinging his arms in wild, senseless motions. I knew God was very angry at me and that I had better leave before my father did something worse.

A lot of what I experienced during this time was blocked out. My girlfriend calls it *selective amnesia*. We remember what we want, and we forget what we want.

Another year passed, and things got even worse. I knew showdown time was finally coming because now my younger sister was getting older and developing breasts, and Daddy started looking at her. I knew that this would be too much to handle, because my younger brothers and sisters were like my children.

In fact, now I know why my mother left. She left because my father was having sex with my two older sisters. She couldn't take it no more and left because of the hurt she was feeling. I know my mother felt powerless to stop my father. But how she could leave her children cold and never talk to them again really puzzles and angers me.

Anyway, I knew it was time to leave, because one night I heard Sharon screaming. "Stop it, Daddy, don't do that to me!"

I jumped up from my bed and grabbed a butcher knife from the kitchen drawer. I ran into Sharon's room screaming, with the butcher knife in my hand. "Don't you touch her, you dirty dog! Take your black hands off my baby! I'll kill you! I'll kill you, don't you touch my baby!"

As I burst into the room with the knife high in my hand, my father jumped up from the bed with a startled and bewildered look on his face and pulled his pants up. This was the first time I ever saw my father afraid. He looked like a wounded animal with signs of caged desperation in his eyes.

"Now, Julia," he said, backing into the corner. "Don't do nothing crazy, Girl! Just keep your cool! Daddy won't hurt you! Daddy's not going to hurt anybody! Just put the knife down before you hurt somebody!"

He started easing towards me with his hand out to take the knife. "If you take one step closer, I'll cut your fricking heart out! Get back before I kill you! I'll kill you. I'll kill you! How dare you touch her! You think because you did it to all of us you can do it to her? You think you can just keep doing this to us without paying for it? I ought to slit your throat right now! I ought to kill you dead right here, you dirty low-life dog!"

I began to let it all loose then. I shouted and screamed at my father, saying all the things I'd been wanting to say for years. I really believe that I would have cut his heart and testicles out with no remorse. It's the first time that I realized that I could have actually killed my father and felt no pain.

I kept screaming, and Sharon wailed, "Julia, please don't kill Daddy. Please don't."

"Listen to her now, Julia," said my father, still standing in the corner, holding his pants up. "Now, don't do nothing foolish!"

"If you say another word...," I said.

"Lord, forgive me," my father moaned, looking toward the ceiling. "You know I didn't mean to hurt nobody," he said plaintively. "I'm sorry, Lord, for hurting my family this way." At that moment my father broke down and yelped like a coyote! He cried so hard that he slid down the wall and just sat limp, weeping like a baby. While he sat in the corner crying, I told Sharon to pack her things, because we were leaving.

We all packed our bags and left in the middle of the night, just like my mother and sisters had done before us. I had already thought about taking the children north to Chicago to stay with some relatives. I had saved the money I had made working in the store, and I bought us all train tickets.

I have since seen my father many times, and he has gotten professional help. My sisters and brothers are doing fine. They've all graduated from college and are doing great. We all still carry baggage, though. The memory of what happened is still there.

I still say that this is the most important single experience that shaped my life and my understanding of who God is and what God's about. I know that if it hadn't been for God, I would probably still be living in an incestuous relationship with my father in Mississippi. I know a lot of people might have a problem with me talking about this—especially men and others who want to say that such things don't happen in black families. The fact that I am able to talk about this means some healing has already taken place. I wish more women would talk about it so they can free themselves from its devastating affects.

My talks with God brought me through. I think about how God got me over. It was the only thing helping me to keep my sanity. I know the Lord is always there, but sometimes we all wonder when we're going through things if God is out to lunch when things are going tough. Of all the things that have happened to me in my life, this experience has been the most important in influencing my relationship with God. I know I'll never go back, but the memories of the pain of what happened to me will always be there as long as I live. I'm still struggling now, but I know that God didn't bring me this far just to leave me. Each day God helps me to get over the pain.

Commentary

I stated earlier that an important aspect of street corner theology is the claim that lived human experience is the primary factor shaping people's understandings of God. The reality of God is not static but often open-ended, wherein individuals struggle to develop definitions, ideas, and feelings about God as their lives unfold. The canons and truths of lived archetypal experiences therefore have more prominent influence in dynamically shaping theology. A key aspect of indigenous black theology is the dynamic, progressive revelation of God in the context of lived human predicaments. God provides resources for healing and recovery amid the terror of personal human relationships. Knowing how and when to respond to the calamities of human circumstances is often revealed as one struggles to know God.

Julia's theology did not evolve from the black church, nor did that of her parents. Yet from this short glimpse into their lives, we see that some semblance of religiosity existed and some understanding of God was formulated. Indigenous black theology is not necessarily cultivated through the prisms of established religion. While the African American church has been instrumental in shaping the theology and religious perspectives of countless African Americans, many blacks have developed personal theologies outside the rich traditions of the black church.

This feature of indigenous black theology is thus based on experiences outside the traditional structures and norms of black religious institutions. While the black church is the predominant influence shaping the religious experience and ethos of African American people, many blacks have developed theologies primarily from the "survival oracles" of African American culture. Such knowledge is principally learned not through the traditional idioms of belief (such as the church, scripture, sermons, or other sacred writings) but from the archives and shrines of black existence and culture which intrinsically develop their own ideas of the sacred, the spiritual, the religious, and the ethical.

Two key elements present in Julia's narrative are definitive aspects of indigenous black theology. First, her understanding of God was shaped through her experience with incest and rape. Indigenous black theology affirms that notions of God have a transcendent character which compel people to exceed barriers to personal growth and transformation. Furthermore, though Julia's story is one of sexual abuse, she did not lose hope in God. She did not become so victimized that she could not spiritually surmount the negative impact of her experiences.

Second, Julia's theology before incest was not fully formulated. She indicates that much of her interpretations of God came prior and subsequent to her traumatic encounters with her father. However, she previously did not have a fully developed concept of God. Not having exposure to scripture and other formative sources, she formulated her understandings from the truths revealed through her lived daily experiences. Her personal theology was developed as a survival mechanism against threats to her own life. Much indigenous street corner theology is survival theology. Opinions, ideas, and realities of God are cultivated to help people live under adverse conditions. This will to live is a hallmark of black culture.

While indigenous theology embraces the notion of the permanency of God, it also affirms that understandings of God are often ever-changing as archetypal human experience unfolds. Julia's theology was not only influenced by her previous, nominal understandings of God but also by what she had come to discover about God during the course of her devastating experience. There must have been some archive of knowledge which imparted to her the central ideas of theological formation. It is my contention that this knowledge was conveyed primarily through the cultural folkways and mores of black life, which instill a sensibility and value for life that empowers individuals to transcend the brutality and meaninglessness of personal circumstances. Indigenous black theology values this reality in the experience of African American people as a formative factor of theological development.

Julia spoke of God coming to her in dreams issuing warnings about stopping her father's sexual defilement. God's revelation is highly personal and relational, and despite these assaults, she believed that God still cared for her. It was during the time of her father's desecration that she began to have real personal encounters with God in dreams and visions. Because of this concern for her personal well-being, God interceded by exhorting her exodus from continued dehumanization. She knew what her father did was wrong but somehow felt powerless to escape.

Incest was the watershed encounter precipitating a deeper awareness of God as a source of refuge and strength. Because her previous understandings were not fully formulated, she was able to grow into or grasp an awareness of God which helped her confront and subsequently transcend her terrible plight.

Julia's story is not unique. There are countless African American women who have been the victims of incest, but theirs is not a theology of the victimized. Often they have been raped by their fathers, step-fathers, brothers, or uncles, but they have struggled to overcome the devastating impact of this abuse. Discussion of these issues has been taboo, and many people believe that such things do not occur in African American communities. The point here is that Julia, despite this awful experience, managed to develop an understanding of God which allowed her to both address her painful condition and overcome its devastating affects. Julia also revealed that her theology had been developed during the course of her experience, which is further corroboration of the dynamic dimensions of African American spirituality that are vital to indigenous black theology. The point is that the black cultural archives of extant truths are just as vital in shaping religious consciousness and theological perspectives as are established religious texts. The context is thus primordial in shaping indigenous belief.

Indigenous black theology is concerned with the full disclosure of those truths which violate, stifle, and ultimately destroy the individual's quest for spiritual fulfillment and empowerment. This requires a full, unadulterated exploration of those realities and impediments of the black experience. In Julia's case, she managed to survive with her dignity and sanity in place. Living with dignity and overcoming the barriers to personal empowerment and wholeness are important hallmarks of indigenous black theology.

Theology in E-flat: Lord of the ——Improvisation——

Winston Churchill Washington, a self-styled street corner philosopher, has studied everywhere from the university of adversity to M.I.T. A world traveler who has spent significant time in Egypt, Ghana, and Mississippi, he is a self-appointed fifty-six-year-old guru of black life in America.

Formerly a student at Julliard School of Music and a Wunderkind at piano, he later dropped out of Julliard to sell Persian rugs on the streets of New York. A superlative student in numerous disciplines, his interest in university life admittedly was never fully sustained. Winston both astounded and baffled his M.I.T. professors with his "significant contribution to the current canons of mathematical science" and his down-home Mississippi Bayou, blues, jazz, and P-funk orientation and disposition.

While brilliantly gifted and highly suspicious of all things orthodox and conventional, Winston is an unapologetic observer of black history, culture, and music. Combining the best of both worlds, he is as ably conversant in the theory and propositions of quantum theory as he is in the oppositional choral structures of free jazz music. He is standing on his corner in Manhattan, selling his rugs, trinkets, and other gadgets. Puffing valiantly and brilliantly on an old church-warden pipe, he recounts his experiences with God between wistful sips of the Jack Daniel's Whiskey that is stashed in his inside coat pocket.

Winston's Narrative

The great Larry Bird of the Boston Celtics once remarked that he thought that Michael Jordan was God in disguise. I felt the same way about Charlie Parker when I was a teenager first hearing him at the Three Deuces in New York. Man, could he wail! I'd heard nothing like him then, and I've seen nothing like him since. I was spellbound, mesmerized by his improvisational techniques, manual dexterity, and the ethereal, heaven-rent reverberations of his phoenix-like lyricism. If anyone was God incarnate, it was Sir Charles the Yard Bird Parker, guru of modern jazz, Brahmin of the brass incantational recitation, mahatma of those refugees of nirvana in the Big Apple seeking moksha from the dirges of swing and the rhapsodies of blue. Seeing the Yard Bird play was like watching God improvise in mid-air, because after he played there was no air left. He sucked all the air out of the joint because all observers where breathless!

What he did with the alto saxophone gave Adolph Sax his final rest. What he did with modern jazz, Einstein did with relativity, Bohr did with physics, and the Colonel did with chicken. God was doing something new when Charlie Parker came on the scene. God had to be in the man for him to achieve what he did.

Studying hard and going to see the Yard Bird play were the only religious things I've ever done in my life. I'm referring to the religion of applied discipline, hard work, and consistency. I never went to church regularly, but going to see the Yard Bird was like being in the sanctuary, in the house of the Lord, watching God do his thing. The phenomenology of his creativity was the linchpin of his anointed status, the sacred founts of his riffs and runs. Chromatic scales and chordal structures will never be the same. The people who heard the man speak through the E-flat instrument of divine inspiration will never be the same. Their lives were touched at their sanctum, at their holy of holies, because each venue with the man was an undertaking of cosmic proportions. "Hosanna, Hosanna, Hosanna in the highest."

What I'm saying is not hyperbole. Exaggeration is not my motive here. Parker has disciples in every corner of the world. No haven or hamlet has been untouched by his music. He was here in a moment and gone in a moment, a meteor flashing brightly but briefly across the vast constellation of humanity. He died young, touching many and redeeming few. The creativity and genius of the Yard Bird represents a discourse on the creative propensities of God. We cannot talk of the creativity of God without discussing the spiritual and corporeal manifestation of the Yard Bird.

God created Parker, and then came the rest of creation. Coming within purview of his horn was a mystical experience. Both the facility and beauty of his playing spoke of other worlds before time was time and man was man. Hearing the music lifted the soul beyond its mortal discord into concordant communion with the Creator. Whoever was down for the count could claim a victory over their opponents after hearing Parker's music. There were times in his playing when people would shout, and there were moments when they were perfectly stilled, enthralled, enraptured, and enamored, awed by the profundity and verbosity of his phraseology.

Elijah Muhammad says that master W.D. Fard was God incarnate. The Rahstahs say his late eminence Haile Selassie was the earthly manifestation of Christ. I say God manifested another creative principle when he came in the form of Charlie Parker. The principle of divine human creativity reached a new apex when the Yard Bird messianically emerged from the blackened and smoke-filled corridors of Kansas City juke joints and New York fly-by-nights.

This idea of God in Charlie Parker's creative genius is no misnomer, for what is God but creative principle? The pinnacle of God's creativity is manifested through the principle of improvisation.

Creating on the moment, without a script, is an essential technique of improvisation. It's also possessing the courage and facility, the freedom and artistry to do something new and innovative, to explore new vistas and create new methodologies to get a message across. The principle of improvisation has always been a strength of African American people. We've always lived improvisationally. The genius of our people is expressed through our ability to give form to function without a holy writ, without a blueprint of how the thing needs to be done. That's what makes us so dangerous—our ability to create something terribly profound on the law of the moment. Modern jazz is an example of that creative principle in music. No other musical forms like it existed. It emerged from the bosom and loins of African American people, coalescing European classical interpretations with African polyrhythmic constructions. The music is unique not simply because of its form and content but because of the principles of improvisation which give it unique character and vitality.

One of the greatest jazz albums of all time is Miles Davis' *Kind of Blue*. Miles said he had the general sketches of the arrangements to be played, but when the group came together to record, most of the music was improvised. This is a classic example of the principle of improvisation at work to create something meaningful, beautiful, and enduring for all time.

The principle of creativity as manifested through the various works of black artists and thinkers is actually the mind of God at work. If anything should be placed on the altars of praise and adulation to God, it's the principle of creativity, which is manifested through all creation but has a particular revelation in the life and culture of African American people.

Even in viewing the reality of God panoramically from the standpoints of nature, science, or art, we cannot fathom its depths without analyzing the creative principles which germinate life. It is impossible to delineate the power, purpose, and purport of God without addressing the issue of creativity.

All life is based on the dynamics of change. The ability of organisms to live and function is predicated on the implementation of positive, progressive change.

In biology and medicine, the principles are called metabolism and catabolism, the regeneration and degeneration of human cells and organisms. Creative transformation permeates all. It is the indispensable stuff of life! Life could not exist without a creative principle.

You see, this is the first law and dynamic of theology. The principle of creativity and its various manifestations give us clues to the nature and mind of God. The God of indigenous experience is certainly a creative principle and has been since long before Tao, Buddha, Mohammed, and Jesus were the reality of the creative force, the élan vital, which compels and comports all creation to its appointed destination.

This is the mind of God, the first order from which all creation evolves. Creativity is the means and manifestation of that order. Improvisation is the *modus operandi* of life's creative movement. The Charlie Parkers and John Coltranes are so profound because their prodigious creativity, which is the mind and manifestation of God doing a new thing in time and space, represents a paradigm shift in their creative art form. Shifts in the axis of subsequent interpretations are compelled by principles of creativity whose primary impetus is improvisation.

Improvisation can follow the spontaneity of the moment or be an outgrowth of rational planning. Charlie Parker improvised on the variations of a particular song, but the innovative paradigm shifts he heralded as a new musical genre were also thoughtfully anticipated. Jazz mutations from swing to be-bop weren't whimsical transpirations but the result of visionaries who portended the transitions through a painstaking and laborious exploration of new ideas. Thus improvisation is both spontaneous and rehearsed, advertent and inadvertent. The imprint of ideas forming the corpus of creativity leads to new canonizations, interpretations, and trajectories of the art form itself. The imprint of the creative idea is the blueprint for the created order.

Whatever your interpretation, the mind of God cannot be comprehended without improvisation, and all life is dependent upon it for vitality. As both the embodiment and proponent of a radical transformation of American classical music, Charlie Parker vaulted the form and substance of modern jazz to new heights. Alfred North Whitehead observed that all Western philosophy was a footnote to Plato. In my opinion, all modern Jazz is a footnote to Charlie Yard Bird Parker.

My analysis here is not apotheosis. The deification of Parker has to do not only with his creative genius, the gifted virtuosity of his playing, or that he was the most privileged purveyor of innovative musical concepts, but with the messianic force of his musical message and the salvific entreaties he made to thousands of the depressed of the post-war generation. Parker's fluid style and flamboyant reedsmanship mirrored an urbane life lived in the fast lane. Art imitates life indeed, and what Parker gave us can never be imitated.

Transcendence, exaltation, freedom of expression, and lived prosperity, however fleeting and ephemeral, were watchwords of countless numbers of African Americans. As spokesperson of the masses, his musical vocabulary was replete with such terminology, and he said with his horn what others could not say with their tongues. He spoke to their dreams. He spoke to their souls. He sublimely articulated their highest aspirations as could only a true messiah. The messianic uplift of his music brought a revivification of souls long lost in the darkened dregs of their nocturnal environs. A new spirit of exhilaration and joy overflowed in the night spots where he played. Winged flight! Endless flight! Spirits liberated! Apocalypse, eclipse, triumvirate bliss! The messiah had come. That which was darkened had come to light. That which stood upright was overturned. Eternity and serenity had come in the backwashes of obscure nightclubs and town taverns. This had to be God, very God, revolutionizing a people through a black bopper from Kansas City.

Can any good thing come out of Kansas City? Would the messiah manifest himself as a gifted musician strung out on dope?

Indigenous black theology, to utilize your vernacular, Doctor, posits the creative mind of God as a first and main principle of life and improvisation the *sine qua non* of creative vitality. Charlie Parker was the epitome of this exquisite gift. There were no predecessors and no heirs to this magnificent throne. The power and effulgence of his improvisation is what liberated the people who saw and heard him.

We cannot understand the God of indigenous black theology as a creative principle without discussing the manifestation of Charles Parker. I can see the professional theologists turning in the chairs, for it is God, they say, who determines the creative principle, not the principle which determines God. Besides, God would not reveal himself in the form of a corpulent black body from Kansas City. God would not do a new thing and speak to souls through the universal language of music. After all, Jesus played no horn and wrote no music. How could we possibly conceive of God in such mundane, frivolous, and ludicrous terms? Many people are just now coming to appreciate Parker's music some forty years after his death. The sacred oracles of his life and work are just being canonized in a unified form. Could it be that, in the words of that great poet Eliot, "we had the experience but missed the meaning?"

The creative principle of God means that God always has the freedom to do a new thing, to improvise with what God has for the moment. The holy grail would not be pursued in the milieu of King Arthur's court by the knights of the nobless noblige, but in the streets of New York City, Paris, Toronto, Detroit, and Chicago by a wandering, drug-addicted waif who could barely keep stride of his E-flat alto.

If creativity is the principal axiom of indigenous black theology, Charlie Parker was the son of God, if not God himself. For we cannot know the day or time that this creative principle will manifest itself in the form of a new creation. We do know that God's improvisation is God's alone, and neither the theologians nor the intellectuals of this society and world can determine the form and substance of that revelation.

Creativity and improvisation are hallmarks of indigenous spirituality, for God is continually revealing and doing new things within and without the created order. It is we human beings who are stuck in the quagmires of orthodoxy and convention, brooking no new sightings, no new ways of seeing and knowing unless corroborated and authenticated by the erudite keepers of those sacrosanct traditions.

African American spirituality has always stood outside of those traditions, because indigenous peoples, the tillers of soils and the reapers of harvest, have understood the creative mind of God to be innovatively at work despite our cognitive constraints. It is indigenous theology of the outsider, the one who comes and goes almost without notice and certainly without the sanctions of the appointed prelates who often creatively and brilliantly make the greatest impact on humanity. They personify the creative principle, which is life itself in every form, valance, and variation. They are manifestations of the mind of God pushing human boundaries away from themselves into newer vistas and thoroughfares of creativity. Their word effects the ultimate liberation of humanity from itself, and their voice heralds the unseen search for new frontiers.

Indigenous peoples have always understood this aspect of God, that the way God chooses to reveal himself is not the office of intellectuals. We are guides along the way, pointing to new possibilities, directing the attention of humanity to places where God is improvising in reality, doing newer, more creative things which enhance both the context and content of our quest for personal and corporate meaning.

Black people in America epitomize this creative, improvisational principle. Not only is American classical music—jazz—the only indigenously created art form in America, but it is emblematic of the creative mind of God working redemptively through those cast aways of outsider status. Black people created jazz. It is a commentary on our lives as outsiders in America. Indigenous black theology values the sanctity of this claim and understands this creative principle to be the mind of God. No other people in America can claim such authorship. The creative mind of God has worked through the unexpected, the least likely to be approved black minds and souls as an improvisational metaphor on the human search for meaning. This aspect of the spirituality of indigenous black theology was formulated long before black people discovered and introduced organized religions to the rest of the world.

The same indigenous theology with its exaltation of the creative mind of God as a first postulate for theological discourse and construction is at work in communities across this nation. Many black people, who are neither Christian, Muslim, Hindu, or Buddhist, have viable and tenable perspectives on the reality of God. Theirs is not a theology of the marketplace. It is not theology fashioned in the workplace of the academy or hallowed halls of university systems. Instead, it is that theology which emerges out of the ethos and culture, the folkways, mores, and lived experiences of African American people. It is real, lived indigenous experience which informs such understandings of God.

People of indigenous persuasion therefore have no problem comprehending both the prophetic and messianic aspects of Charlie Parker's music, because they understand God as a creative, improvisational spirit and music as a harmonizing force in the chaos of reality. Such evaluation can never be embraced by the Christo-centric theology of Euro-American society because it is counter to prevailing interpretations about the way God has revealed himself through historical processes. God could never be commensurate with creative principle. But for those whose theological understandings and spiritual sensibilities embrace a wide range of possibilities often incongruous with traditional dogmas, such interpretation is not remote.

This evaluation of Charlie Parker's music is not mere poppycock. He is a manifestation of the highest form of this creative principle which is the foundation of indigenous thought. The fact that he died from a drug overdose does not belie the magnanimity and efficacy of his creative genius. His crucible was that despite his genius and creative profundity, as a black man in America he was still an outsider. The significance and brilliance of his work would never be accepted or appreciated by the larger culture, because that culture is forever stymied by its own presuppositions and formulas concerning how things are to be interpreted and what methods should be employed to convey such analysis. Unless these new and creative ideas fall within previously established configurations of thought or are disseminated by people who are acceptable, they are seldom celebrated or revered as products of lasting worth.

Black indigenous life both values and exalts experiences falling outside the purview of the larger culture. Jazz is a testament to that creative, improvisational experience which is expression that is oppositional to the conventions and sacrandas of the larger society. It is in this spirit that the indigenous black person embraces reality, finds his sanity, and makes his contribution to world civilization. Improvisation is essential to true spiritual experience and is key to the liberation of those souls sequestered and beleaguered by the antiseptic formalities of the larger culture. Oppression often comes in the form of convention. Improvisation is an antidote to the oppressive process of routinization.

It all begins with the understanding of God as creative principle. Improvisation is freedom to step outside the status quo and create something of value which might free the status quo. If God is anything to indigenous black people, God is creative, innovative, and improvisational. This means that no one can determine the manner and matter in which God is to do his thing except the person or instrument God chooses at a given moment. Charlie Parker was a world historical manifestation of this principle, of God doing a new thing through and among outsiders, bringing a new message of hope and freedom to the despised and rejected. What he did through his music was an artistic simulation of what the people desire to do in reality—order the chaos of their lives, create, and be free.

Improvisation is the personified freedom of the human spirit amid the debilitating constraints and restraints of modern reality. The improviser is the supreme embodiment of the value of freedom. He or she is keeper of those extant truths which are often obviated and obscured by the impediments of tradition. In indigenous black experience, the improviser is representative of the mind and spirit of God breaking through those intransigent customs of the social order. He is an emblem of hope, a bastion of the spirit of freedom, and a citadel of resolve, dash, and courage.

Improvisation is the freedom of the mind of God to do something new through the vehicle of God's choosing. According to the indigenous viewpoint, that vehicle will invariably be one who is repudiated, one who is outside the established parameters of the acceptable and chosen principle.

All this may sound strange, Rev, but it really encapsulates the central propositions of the indigenous understanding.

As a scientist, I value the thorough scrutinization of method. As an artist, I know the importance of form. The God of the indigenous black experience must be revealed through the creative, improvisational process. Otherwise, you and I wouldn't be here having this conversation. The key to our survival and struggle as a people has been our understanding of God as the creator of improvisational capacities for the outsider. Improvisation, more than anything else, personifies the mind of God at work in creation. It is here that all human possibilities are realized and all life comes to its appointed purpose. Until we grasp the meaning of this viewpoint, we can never comprehend the basic tenets of indigenous black theology or fathom how God could use the likes of Yard Bird Parker to be an exponent of the creative change he invariably comports to us. If God is God, he is definitely Lord of the improvisation.

The trouble with humankind is that because God has creatively revealed himself in certain ways in the past, the same revelation of

God is projected for the future. Any prospective analysis of God's manifestation is thereby conditioned by previous retrospective interpretation. Such analysis eradicates any improvisational element in God's freedom to reveal himself in different forms.

Indigenous black peoples have always been open to the revelation of God in different ways, but the consistent element through all such manifestations is the creative, improvisational principle, the mind of God choosing to do a new thing in creation. Because of our historical conditioning, we often miss God's true purpose for our lives because we are anticipating something entirely different than what God discloses.

The gift of indigenous peoples is that spiritually we have always grasped the fundamental meaning of this reality. The gift of indigenous black theology is that it posits this as a central axiom of faith.

Notice I said "we" in identifying indigenous peoples. My university training does not preclude me from claiming myself as an indigenous person. My beliefs incorporate the fundamental values and precepts of indigenous thought. It is not where you have been trained that makes you of indigenous persuasion but the nature of the beliefs you hold to be representative of indigenous values.

Woe Bop Shabbam, baby, there it is, theology in E-flat!

Commentary

Winston's analysis of the God of indigenous experience as creative, improvisational principle captures a central proposition of indigenous black theology. The idea of God as creative principle has been understood by black people for thousands of years. In fact, a common element of African and African American indigenous theologies is the improvisational and creative capacities of God to shape creation according to specific designs.

This motif pervades every aspect of life itself. In nature, improvisational changes congeal and disburse in newer, more creative life forms. In biology, it is realized in organisms moving to complete themselves. In political and social processes, the transfiguration of old orders culminate in the formation of new systems of governance and belief. The creative mind of God is continually transforming human existence through improvisational patterns. The preeminent expression of that creative principle is realized in the inventive individual who becomes the penultimate culmination of the mind of the deity.

As outsiders to the American experience, African Americans have always relied on improvisation as a technique for existence and survival. This principle is not only manifested in science and art but in the creative ways black people through daily experience have historically and contemporaneously impacted the culture around them. Black life on the plantation and black life today in America could not have evolved without an improvisational impulse, a spirit which values the freedom to do something new amid the old moorings, proscriptions, and prohibitions of the larger society.

It is axiomatic that the spirit of freedom is embodied in the capacity and courage to improvise. Where bodies were enslaved, spirits were free to create and interpret according to the mind of God and the laws of the moment. This basic ability to freely create and improvise is one of the central differentiating factors of indigenous black theology from all other theologies. It has been both paramount and indispensable to the struggle for survival and authentic existence in African American life.

Various people throughout African American history have thus personified the archetype of improvisational creativity. They are paragons of this creative mind of God revealing itself in the context of lived human experience. Indigenous black theology has always venerated the lives of such people as individual expressions of the collective struggle for freedom. Such valuations have always exceeded, interceded, and succeeded the claims of mainstream religions. Before Christianity and other world religions existed, there were indigenous black perspectives whose legitimacy and value have always rested on their authors' experiences as outsiders. The authentic nature of indigenous perspectives can be largely ascribed to their authors' status as social pariahs. The freedom to do a new thing, to create and improvise, is thus largely due to this spirit of determination to transcend those barriers strewn in their paths.

Winston makes a brilliant observation about the subtle and iconoclastic manner in which the creative proclivities find expression in the African American experience. Charlie Parker's representing the creative mind of God and personifying a central tenet of indigenous black theology is a fact which appears preposterous, if not altogether demented. But those fathoming the true angularities of Winston's vision can fully understand the point he is trying to convey.

Since for indigenous black people God is creative principle revealing himself or herself in ways anomalous to the currents of convention, the idea of Yard Bird being a creative manifestation of the indigenous deity is not far-fetched. The fact that Yard Bird made a revolutionary impact in an idiom which is America's only indigenously created art form further corroborates the authenticity of this claim. If music is a harmonizing force of nature also reflecting the mind and will of God, as indigenous black theology affirms, then the creative manifestation of Charlie Parker's genius is a testament to this reality.

God of the
──Healthy Body──

Chausiku Zuwena, a sixty-two-year-old black woman from Chicago, is married with three children and seven grandchildren. Chausiku studies herbal medicine and nutritional healing and therapy, and she specializes in acupuncture and the science of Naturopathy. She is tall and lean, with radiant black skin and brown eyes. Her regal propriety and graceful disposition are reminiscent of African royalty. A frequent traveler to the "Motherland of Alkebulan," she is filled with the wisdom and love of her people.

After teaching public school for thirty-five years, she retired to establish Motherland Nutritional Counseling and Naturalistic Healing Services, Inc. in Chicago. A wonderful storyteller with the gift for "painting" vivid pictures, she is a woman of strength, dignity, and determination. She is the first of twelve children born in St. Louis to parents who were day laborers. Her father died at age forty-two of cardiac failure and her mother passed at age fifty from breast cancer.

Chausiku attributes the premature death of her parents to a lifetime of poor eating and has devoted her life to restoring the health of African American people. She says, "Our poor health is the chief nemesis of our downfall and discomfiture as a race." Here is her story.

Chausiku's Narrative

I can tell much about the health of my people by just looking into their eyes. The eyes tell all about our state of health, and when I look at us, my heart is saddened. We have come a long way from the days of sun on the plantations to our present time in history. Then, we lived off poor food but managed to work off its adverse affects in the fields. The detrimental impact of poor nutrition has plagued us for years, and we can see the results in swollen ankles, arthritis, and other maladies which continue to kill us before we've lived fully. I can see the generations of poor nutrition in the faces of my people. We still have not changed our diet since the days of slavery. Now we eat more processed and chemically laden foods than ever before. In fact, today we are much worse off than our ancestors because of our sedentary and high-stress lifestyles.

Have you ever looked deeply into the eyes of our people? Have you ever taken a long look at us? Our body posture, the way we carry our bodies, says much about how we truly feel on the inside. How we feel has much to do with what and when we eat. Too many of us have diseases and afflictions which can be prevented through the proper nutrition. The high blood pressure so prevalent in our people can be attributed to diets high in sodium and fat. We don't ever have to worry about other people killing us. We kill ourselves by the things we put into our bodies. We are generally in poor health because we do not care for our bodies as we should. We don't eat the proper foods, get appropriate rest, or adopt those measures which ensure optimum health.

We must care for the life God has given us. The most important gift from the Creator are these wonderful bodies. The body is so remarkable. It has all the healing properties within it and has amazing resiliency against incessant abuse. We must use our minds, hearts, and the wisdom of ancient spirits to guide us in the right decision-making to care for ourselves. By taking care of these magnificent temples of creation, we are acknowledging the goodness of this gift.

Indigenous black spirituality includes the development of practices which teach the proper care of our bodies and spirits. We believe that wholesome spirituality involves a steady diet of spiritual and physical food. To become the best for God, we must spend more time caring for ourselves in ways which will bring God glory and praise.

One of my main criticisms of Christianity (except the Seventh Day Adventists) is the omission of precepts on physical nutrition as an integral component of spiritual wholeness and wellness. A positive aspect of Christianity is its emphasis on fasting and cleansing the body to increase spiritual awareness. A negative aspect is the absence of any sound, systematic doctrine which teaches proper nutrition and bodily care as a basis for developing spiritual consciousness.

The Adventists strongly value the vegetarian diet and the avoidance of those foods with chemical additives. But very few other denominations, sects, or faiths, other than those of the Eastern variety, underscore the importance of physical and spiritual health as a foundation for higher spiritual awareness. They encourage moving closer to God by studying the Word and engaging in those disciplines which strengthen the spirit while ignoring the body. This is a contradiction. Maximum positive spirituality affirms programs which teach people to do both—study the Word for spiritual strength and eat the correct foods for physical vitality.

The Christian faith could be positively enhanced by emphasizing these claims. If more people practiced positive, long-term nutrition and therapy as a part of their spirituality, they would live longer and healthier lives. God certainly wants this for all of her people, and we need more training in this area.

The late Ellen White wrote some significant tracts on the importance of Christians balancing their spiritual and physical diets with the proper nutrition. Few others have followed her lead.

This notion of physical nutrition as being essential to spiritual vitality is a foundational principle of African indigenous spirituality. The problem with Western spirituality is that it makes no provisions for the human diet. Part of this problem may be ascribed to the basic ideas informing the practice of religion in the West. Christianity is largely shaped by Western psychology, which has defined the human person in terms of psyche—mind only.

The Greek idea of psyche, borrowed from their mentors, the Nile Valley Africans, purported the totality of the individual person, which included mind, body, and spirit. Spirituality, whose foundation is psyche, addresses the needs of the total person and not simply the mind, as the Europeans have professed.

Indigenous black spirituality from the time of Egypt until the present in America addresses the needs of the complete person as a means of spiritual enlightenment. We therefore cannot develop a full-blown, comprehensive spiritual program without considering the whole person. Our understanding of God embraces the notions of health, vitality, and personal and communal healing. The most important gift to us is our health.

The God we worship and serve is a God of health, healing, and wellness. God's primary objective for her people is to maintain their optimum health, wholeness, tranquillity and serenity. Without health, all life is devalued. Nothing is more important to us, and nothing is taken for granted more than our health.

You will note, Brother, that I refer to God as *she*, for the feminine principle is the parental fount of all spirituality in life. Healing involves two primary ideas: mending that which is broken and soothing that which has been hurt. The health and healing bases of all progressive spirituality from a black indigenous standpoint view the reality of God as a feminine principle.

The primary vehicle for nurturing, healing, mending, and soothing is the feminine. While God may ultimately personify both male and female, the primary attribute for wholeness, vitality, and health is female. No other force in nature or reality works to mend, heal, and console as does the feminine reality. In African traditional society this is true. In the indigenous, grass roots experience of African Americans, it is also true.

We see the feminine attributes of God at work through the healing process—a process revealed in every aspect of creation. We see the two principles of male and female at work on every level of the created order. In nature, we see evidence of the masculine principle working through cosmic gales and strong winds. Wherever power manifests itself in this coercive way, the masculine is present.

Through processes of healing, rejuvenation, and restoration of human bodies, minds, and souls, the feminine principle is at work. I believe that the healing aspect of the reality of God is a feminine principle, and long before the advent of patriarchal authority in European society, African and other Eastern cultures revered the role and responsibility of the feminine sex in the formation and restitution of human society.

The religions of ancient cultures venerated women and many of the Gods were of female gender. Not until the emergence of Hebraic and Western civilization did the female experience a subordination of rights, privileges, and basic personhood. Many of the archaeological discoveries of the eighteenth and nineteenth centuries by the British and French labeled the religions of the east and their female deities as *cults* because of the general denigration of women in those societies. The only legitimate world religions, from a European standpoint, were those with male deities.

Without sounding sexist here, I want to say that man has a gift for making war, wreaking havoc, and spilling blood. The female person has always had a vital role in the restoration of society subsequent to the ravages of war. Without the presence of the female person, the health and rejuvenation of societies and peoples would be difficult to achieve, particularly in times of war and disillusionment. Women have always been the primary healers within a given society.

Although women have not functioned primarily as clergy and physicians, who are revered vocationally as the principal healers in

Western society, they have had a definitive role in healing and maintaining the most vital institution in society—the family. Women have always been the predominant, unofficial healers of society on every level, and this fact cannot be overlooked. They do the work physicians and clergy cannot do. They mend, heal, and soothe the broken-hearted and disconsolate between visits to church and the doctor's office.

For me, this is the most vital healing of all, healing which allows people to hold their lives together. They heal their minds and spirits, both of which are important dimensions of people's health. Without this female or mother principle, humankind could not eugenically realize its greatest human potential. The female gender is indispensable to the human healing and restoration process.

The indigenous black viewpoint embraces the God of health and healing as a feminine principle. There is no shame in postulating this concept, because human beings act out this belief on a deeper, subconscious level. To whom do children primarily turn when they need comfort, love, healing, and tender understanding? This does not deny the opportunity of men to take on this responsibility, but the feminine principle of healing is widely manifested through everything from our behavior to the way we respond to crisis situations.

In examining the religions of the world, one invariably discovers at their core this desire that humans have for wholeness, healing, and the realization of maximum personal potential through a positive relationship with God. From Christianity to Islam, the principle of healing—which is the mother principle—resides at their core. Although the organizers and prophets of those religions have primarily been men, their underlying proposition and precepts speak to the refurbishment of the human souls and hearts which have been ravaged. They address the human need for healing and establish their teachings around ways in which this convalescence may best occur. Muslims turn to Allah, the beneficent and merciful. Christians embrace Christ, the Son of God. Jews affirm the law and prophets, the majesty and power of Yahweh, Elohim, and Adonai. Despite the employment of male deities, all religions have at their center the feminine principle of healing and spiritual rehabilitation.

I mentioned earlier that physical healing should be an essential part of any viable spirituality. We cannot discuss true spirituality by ignoring the food we eat and the abuse of our bodies. We simply cannot realize our maximum spiritual potential without eating the proper foods and getting the appropriate rest and exercise.

The fundamental objective of all spirituality is human wholeness. This sense of completion and consummation cannot be reached if people ignore and abuse their bodies. True spiritual vitality cannot occur when our bodies are replete with toxic substances that bring on the illnesses and maladies which plague us. The only beneficiaries of a lifetime of poor eating are health professionals and hospitals. You've heard the old adage that we live off half of what we eat, and the doctors live off the other half. This is true! Many of our health problems could be eradicated through a change in consciousness which would effect a positive transformation of spiritual and physical lifestyle.

Everything we need for growth, development, and good health has been given to us by God through natural substances. Fruits, vegetables, nuts, and whole grains are the things of the earth that God has provided for our healing, sustenance, and life. These foods contain the living enzymes and ingredients which promote maximum nutritional vitality and possess properties that facilitate human growth and rejuvenation. God always wants the best for us. She wants us to make the proper choices for the prolongation of human life, our most precious gift. To abuse our bodies the way we do is an insult to the Creator herself.

Not only has God provided the foods and substances for life, but she has given us bodies which have remarkable restoration and healing properties within them. If the mother principle were not contained within the human body itself, we would have perished centuries ago through nutritional and physical abuse.

75

Indigenous spirituality highly accentuates the principles of healing and proper nutrition. This theology dates back thousands of years to when Africans developed a cooperative relationship with nature and viewed the earth and creation as the fundamental source of human well-being. Unlike European societies, with their harsh weather and environmental adversities that created an antagonistic attitude towards nature and earth, Africans developed a more harmonious understanding of God and nature, largely based on a clement climate.

I might add that in all fairness to the Europeans, their culture and civilization might not have flourished without viewing nature as something to be conquered and harnessed. Had they taken a more passive stance towards it, they might not have realized the magnificent achievements of the present day.

The problem is that we today are living with the biological and environmental fallout of Western civilization's battle with nature. Everything from cancer to the AIDS epidemic is symptomatic of a disparaging proliferation of malignant neglect in Western culture. Sure, medical science has tried desperately to develop treatments which will redeem and save us, but it cannot teach us new attitudes about the stewardship of responsibility in properly caring for our bodies, minds, and spirits. The recent fitness craze is a response to decades of nutritional and physical abuse. However, fitness is not synonymous with healthiness, and that's where many of us are highly confused.

A middle-aged man came to see me three years ago. He was highly fit. He worked out in the gym five times a week and had the body of a gladiator. Yet he was unhealthy. He had high blood pressure and colon problems. Now, after two years of nutritional therapy and other interventions, he is now healthy and fit. No more high blood pressure or colon problems. By changing his diet, he overcame the negative impact of years of physical abuse through inadequate nutrition. These techniques are not new. They are as old as God herself. God has given us the things we need for maximum health. We have gotten away from those things through a negation of common sense. My father used to say, "We talk of common sense, but common sense is not common." How true this is.

We must understand that everything in creation is working towards healing, restoration, or ultimate dissolution. We can enhance or thwart this process by what we eat. The most important aspect of the God of indigenous experience is her healing capacities and dimensions. This is fundamentally the most important principle of life itself: healing, health, and human vitality. Without it, all life pales in significance and value.

The ultimate objective of God's plans for our lives is that each of us has health, wholeness, and happiness. This is the first law of spirituality—that we need to take care of ourselves so that we are the best we can be. This means eating the proper foods and getting the appropriate rest, both of which will influence the cultivation of the proper attitude about life. Any comprehensive program of restitutive spirituality must include systematic programs for spiritual and physical vitality.

Why haven't more African American churches addressed this problem? Why doesn't the Christian faith emphasize this more so that more people may engage in activities which inspire good health rather than the reverse? The problem is that Christian spirituality does not accentuate the importance of holistic nutrition and preventive physical care as an essential component of faith. You can eat whatever you want and do whatever you want to yourself, because even after sinfully abusing your body, you can take it to God in prayer and *he* will make everything all right. Instead of teaching preventive physical care as an essential component of spiritual development, the body is omitted—except for the fulfillment of sensual desires. And even here one must be careful not to obtain too much enjoyment.

Optimum spiritual nutrition requires the maximum discipline. In a culture that subliminally seduces people into destructive behavior through continuous advertisement, true physical discipline is difficult to attain.

One of the greatest struggles of vegetarians is to remain so in a culture that encourages the consumption of meat. It's like swimming up Niagara falls. It is extremely difficult to develop a lifestyle of optimum health and vitality when the larger culture is in opposition to it.

It is more important for advertisers and companies to get rich than to promote the truth about their products. If my company produces Fritos, then it is important that I sell as many Fritos as I can. Forget that they might contain elements harmful to your health. Forget that they may be of little nutritional value. The consumption of Fritos has more to do with making someone else rich than obtaining optimum nutrition for my body.

Dick Gregory was correct in arguing that we must differentiate between real food and something to eat. They are two different things.

So God is truly about healing, health, and human restoration. Our understanding of God and human spirituality must embrace the care and nurturing of our bodies as well as the care and nurturing of our minds and spirits. They all interface and are vitally connected to each other.

I decided to dedicate my life to God by healing others and helping as many people as possible to restore their health. Since I believe that the primary attribute of God is that of healer and restorer and that all life reflects this process in creation, we must also embody those principles in our daily living.

Human health is the most important gift God has bestowed on us. All other principles of life revolve around this one foundational fact. Human health and healing are the keys to everything in life. They are the very things on which all life critically depends. Accordingly, the indigenous viewpoint affirms the reality of God as healer, and most of the creative energies of God are expended in this restoration process.

On another level, we see this healing process not only in creation and nature but in human relationships as well. All life seems to struggle to restore that which has been broken and hurt to full wholeness and vitality. Many people today are in need of all types of healing—emotional, psychological, physical, and spiritual. Even relationally, all things revolve around the struggle of individuals to restore themselves in those areas.

Why do people lash out and commit heinous crimes, and why is there so much estrangement and alienation among the human race? If you look carefully at each situation, invariably you will discover the need to heal somewhere in the scenario. Perhaps a person has been wronged by another and seeks spiritual restoration. Or maybe a person has done something which has brought trouble upon himself. His struggle is for wholeness, comfort, healing, and the restitution of his humanity. God is consistently finding ways of applying the healing balm to our minds, bodies, hearts, and spirits.

A basic tenet of indigenous spirituality is the acclamation of God as healer in the universe. The basic objective of indigenous spirituality is the establishment of inward harmony and peace with God through various healing processes. The proper foods heal the body. The proper words heal the mind. The proper attitude heals relationships, and the proper behavior heals all of creation. This is a fundamental ingredient of indigenous black spirituality because God is primarily the feminine principle of healing, and we see her manifestation everywhere. Thank God for this dimension of life, and we pray that each of us will discover the healing gift God has given us for the restoration of ourselves and all of life around us.

Commentary

Indigenous black theology affirms the reality of God in the form of various healing processes. People strive for human wholeness, which is consummated through spiritual, psychological, and physical healing. A certain vitality is experienced by those who pursue spirituality holistically.

Indigenous perspectives recognize the presence of the healing principle in all of creation. The establishment of personal and communal harmony and spiritual equilibrium is actualized by the individual's diligent pursuit of truth, which culminates in the embodiment of a specific lifestyle whose principal objective is spiritual holism. Although Chausiku has framed her indigenous understanding of God as the feminine principle seeking the restoration of human wholeness through optimum nutrition and personal care and healing, the idea has profound implications for those social aggregates pursuing harmony and well-being on the communal level.

At the core of the black experience in America is the need for well-being, wholeness, healing, and personal revitalization. Since this is the primary paradigm of concern for African Americans, the idea of God must facilitate the attainment of this ideal. We cannot fathom the depths of concern for black people in America without addressing the need for personal healing. All notions of spirituality must address this fundamental need. The problem is that blacks have pursued healing through political and economic processes without understanding that those lifestyle choices and behaviors on a personal level are just as important in the restitution of human vitality as those redressed in the halls of Congress.

In other words, the deep and abiding need for black people to attain and retain a sense of wholeness and spiritual vitality cannot be achieved through the political process alone. Indigenous spirituality, then, teaches that healing is indispensable to personal well-being and that such objectives might be attained through something as mundane as the food we put into our bodies, which affects the way we think, behave, and fathom reality. Such choices on a microcosmic level are just as vital to indigenous spirituality as the larger collective processes which confer wholeness to groups macrocosmically through the dissemination of justice. Always at the center of concern is mending that which has been broken and soothing that which has been hurt.

Indigenous black theology embraces the notion of God as healer. The manifestation of this principle may appear in the form of those individuals possessing the gift of human restoration or those intra- and extra-creative processes in nature which move all life toward completion and fulfillment. Thus, the primary work and objectives of God are based upon the feminine principle that all humans must achieve wholeness and that all life processes move to this ultimate consummate purpose.

One problem with Western spirituality and the traditional African American church from Chausiku's viewpoint is the absence of personal responsibility in proactively promoting and enhancing personal vitality through diet and nutrition. People should take responsibility for the state and condition of healing in their own lives. The church should take a stronger role in teaching people the lifestyle choices for optimum nutrition. This cannot occur without a radical change in theology. Rather than reactively pray to God to heal sicknesses which often can be proactively prevented through the proper dietary and lifestyle changes, each person could become more actively involved in therapeutic processes, thereby enhancing his or her own sense of personal well-being. Instead of viewing God as one who invocationally responds to sickness, God becomes an active co-participant in the preventive process through appropriate individual choices which facilitate optimum well-being and wholeness.

The idea of God as healer is an important concept in African traditional theology and African American indigenous theology. It is both a reality and a metaphor for the larger purposes and intent of God in creation. The reality of God as healer is perhaps the most prominent theme in African American spirituality. Whether Christian, Muslim, or indigenous, the central concepts and precepts of these faiths include provisions for the restoration of human vitality by taking care of our bodies.

Christians affirm Jesus as the primary mediator of healing for humanity. The Black Muslims recognize Allah as the primary dispenser of justice and human equality to those victimized by racism and oppression. The indigenous viewpoint affirms the reality of God in the principle of human restoration and regeneration.

That process may culminate in the work of individuals or in the work of nature itself. The irrefutable argument in indigenous theology is that God has implemented a design in nature which moves all life to its appointed dissolution or integration. The integration or the dissolution cannot transpire without the regenerative, unitizing process which holds and sustains life together. For Chausiku and those of the indigenous viewpoint, this foundational principle which undergirds all of creation is spiritual healing and vitality which by their very nature compel and impel all persons to their higher purpose in God.

People must struggle for the mastery of those rules of self-discipline and order which reinforce the hegemony of optimum choices and maximize personal wellness and vitality. Spiritual wellness and wholeness for black people in America cannot be defined solely in terms of social processes but must include a concern for individual responsibilities in making the correct decisions for personal healing and well-being. The indigenous paradigm of spirituality includes these two realities.

God Who
Makes a Way
—Out of No Way—

Abraisha Honeycutt is a homeless person who periodically stays at the Detroit Rescue Mission. She has been without work for three years after her termination from General Motors as a quality control inspector. She is forty-eight years old, college educated, and multi-talented. Her friends call her the "Bag Lady."

She is dressed in a black workman's uniform, a faded, urine-stained, ankle-length gray and black tweed overcoat, black combat boots, and a red ski cap. Her thin, angular fingers and nails painted with chipped red polish protrude from black leather gloves covering the palm of her hands. She is sipping black coffee from a tattered white styrofoam cup and inhaling long and wistfully from a Virginia Slims cigarette between vengeful bites of a Zack's Coney Island dog. She is seated at the refuge counter of the Athenaeum Coney Dog House. This is her story. It is mid-day.

Abraisha's Narrative

It's very unusual for people in my condition to even have an opinion of God. Most folks by now would have just plain given up on the idea that God exists. But you'd be surprised at the number of homeless people like myself who still believe in a supreme being, still have just a little faith left. People think 'cause your body is homeless, your spirit is homeless. But that's just all the more reason why I've got to have a place of refuge for my spirit. My body might be walking these tired streets, but my mind and spirit and soul are always somewhere else. I'm here, but I'm not here. You dig where I'm coming from?

God still speaks to me, and I know I'm not alone. I've been in a lot of dangerous situations which really tried me personally. After first losing my job, I became very depressed. Then came the overdue notices and the eviction papers. Then the unemployment checks which finally ran out. The next thing I knew I was out on the streets with nowhere to go. It was very hard for me, becoming one of the homeless. You tell yourself that that's something that happens to other people, but not you, you know?

Since I've been out here, I've had a lot of dangerous situations come up on me. Men and women trying to take advantage of me by taking my clothes while I'm sleeping and snatching my bags 'cause they think I got some food hidden in them. I want to tell you that it's rough out here, but in every situation God seems to step in and make a way out of no way.

The strange thing about these streets is that they can be very cruel when people get desperate, but there is a humanity out here that an outsider just doesn't see. It ain't all bad. Many of the people out here are just like me. They just fell on hard times, and the next thing they knew, they too were out on the streets. It can happen to anybody. Riding high in April, shot down in April. One minute you're succeeding, the next minute you're pleading. There's a lot of crime and a lot of evil out here, but people who are in the same condition can reach out and help each other in times of real need. You'd be surprised. It ain't all dog-eat-dog!

I remember when I found a sleeping place in one of the alleys in the Cass corridor. It was kind of comfortable. I made a makeshift pallet out of some carpet foam that had been thrown out, and I lay down for a much-needed sleep after miles of walking. Then suddenly I was rushed by a man who started beating me with a crow bar.

As I put my hands and arms to my head to cushion the force of the blows, I saw some hands reach up and snatch the crow bar from the man and start whipping him from behind. I could hardly see because blood was all on my face, but as I was getting up, I saw two women, also homeless, who had come to my rescue. Who else could that have been but God? If those two women had not chased that man away and given him some of his own medicine, I wouldn't be sitting here talking with you now.

I have had several experiences where just in the nick of time somebody—a stranger—showed up and helped me out. I know that's God looking out for me.

One of the things I do out here to get by is read the palms and futures of people. The little change I get from reading people—and that's all it is, change—I take to the restaurant to buy breakfast. My favorite breakfast is always raisin toast and coffee. I don't just get plain toast, but raisin toast! Top of the line toast! Toast fit for a queen! And when I take them long, hard bites, I feel like I used to feel when I was working and making a living. I never thought something as little as small bites of raisin toast two or three times a week would make me happy. I remember the days when bread would rot on top of my refrigerator. Because I had the money, I'd just go and buy more bread. I didn't even eat raisin toast then. Bread had no real meaning for me then because I could get it like we breathe air. But now? Oh, it's a whole different story. To treat myself to raisin toast is a gift from God. There have been times when I was so hungry I was dizzy, but somehow I would manage to get a little pocket change together and end up at Satin's restaurant to set myself down for some raisin toast.

I recall one day when I was so tired after hours of walking and wandering, and I found two dollars in the street. It must have fallen out of somebody's pocket. I went to Satin's and sat down and ordered myself some raisin toast. I sat there for two and a half hours, slowly chewing and savoring the taste of that toast. It was one of the coldest days of winter, but that two dollars allowed me to go and sit down in someplace warm. That day I made three separate orders of toast, all in a row. God made a way out of no way on orders of raisin toast! I was grand that day! I sat myself down at that table like I was sho' 'nuff royalty!

By sitting in that restaurant I was able to unthaw. I was almost frostbitten. You might say that that two dollars saved my life. The owners of the restaurant knew that I was trying to get warm. They could have asked me to leave but didn't. God worked through their kindness. The fact that they didn't put me out was the grace of God.

I can keep telling you about little things like that. Situations where I found my back against the wall and God somehow provided an opening, some daylight in the midst of darkness. God is always making a way out of no way, and that's what keeps me going.

It seems like God works on different time tables. Sometimes she takes a long time coming. I'm just about to give up and give out, but just in a moment's notice, she shows up for the rescue. There's been times when her action was swift and deliberate. Other times she's moving at a snail's pace. But she always makes the way when no way can be seen, found, or heard in the vicinity.

I also remember when I had become so depressed that I was going to drink some Liquid Plumber I found in a dumpster. I had decided to end it all. I was sick that I had lost my job, my house, my family, and my friends. But just as I was opening the bottle to drink it down, a homeless brother handed me a leaflet out of nowhere and then disappeared. It read, "Did you know that Jesus was among the unemployed? Have hope, Brothers and Sisters!"

Now, why would he hand me that leaflet out of the clear blue? It was almost as if God was saying, "Don't do it!" When I read those words, I knew they were meant for me. I knew God was speaking to me through what I call the "flyer from nowhere."

Was that an accident? Was that just something that happened by chance? I happened to be in the right place at the right time?

When I saw those words, I fell on my knees and cried like a motherless child. How could it be that I could be in this predicament but that God would still speak to me?

When it first happened, the most devastating thing for me about being homeless was remembering how things used to be. Knowing I once had a good-paying job and remembering those good times compared to the pain and suffering of the present was enough to drive me to drink Liquid Plumber.

A lot of people suffer deeply, not simply because of their impoverished conditions, but because they somehow can't escape the memory of how good it used to be. It's their memory of the good times and what they once were that always haunts them like a terrible nightmare. The taste of how it was drives them to end it all.

I refuse to let the memory of how it used to be drive me into spiritual poverty and defeat. I don't care how terrible it becomes for me out here. Just reading that leaflet turned my whole life around and helped change my attitude about my present condition. No longer would the beautiful memories of the past destroy my ability to live now with what I have, nor would they destroy my confidence in the future. I live from moment to moment. I try not to think back to the good old days too much. I don't want the memories of yesterday to erase what I'm facing today.

All this sounds pretty wild, don't it? But that's the way I feel. God is making a way out of no way through little things.

As a homeless person, I see things I never saw before. My mind is much more attuned to little things. I pay much closer attention to things, particularly on the ground. So much of my day is spent walking and looking down that I notice everything that's on the ground. You would not believe the amount of money I have found on the ground. Things other people walk by and don't even notice, I pick up with just the scanning of my eyes. That song "Down Here on the Ground" has special meaning for me.

My awareness of things is much keener than it's ever been. Not too much escapes me. I've even mastered bird watching. Before becoming homeless, I never paid attention to the sounds of birds. But now I can sit in the park and listen and hear them sing and sometimes anticipate what rhythms of singing will come next. What I'm saying sounds crazy, but it's true!

How many little things do you notice on any given day? How keen is your awareness? Having a lot of possessions conditions the way we see the world around us, but *not* having things conditions how we perceive our world, too. Big things condition us to see the big picture. Little things help us to appreciate the little picture, things most people don't ordinarily see.

You ever thought about that? Because of my situation and condition, I have developed a whole new way of seeing that I never had before, and that's a blessing from God.

Many people go through life without ever truly seeing the things around them. Their whole outlook on life is conditioned by the experiences they've had or the information passed on to them by other people. They never truly see things through their own eyes, and this is the real tragedy of human experience.

Yes, being homeless has taught me a whole new way of seeing things. I pay attention to the little things which make the biggest difference in life. There are things in this city, like landmarks, places, and buildings that I never would have noticed had I not been homeless. I'm not justifying not having a home. I am only saying that we miss so much of life because we don't take the time to see what's around us. God helps us to see the little things, and by seeing the little things, we grasp the details of God's handiwork in creation.

I know every nook and cranny of some neighborhoods. I have places to sleep, comfortable places the rest of the world knows nothing about. Yes, I walk the streets. Yes, times are very, very tough. But there are places of refuge where I can go and hide out from the rest of the world. They are places that only other homeless people know about. It's like being in the belly of a whale.

So I have an advantage in a sense. Most people don't have places where they can hide out and where nobody knows where they are.

There is a certain comfort in knowing that I can escape from the world when I want to and that nobody will ever know where I am.

This probably sounds strange to you. Most people couldn't see how homelessness could give them an advantage in any circumstance. If they came looking for me tomorrow, they'd never find me, because they would never know where to look. I'm one up on everybody else by virtue of this condition and situation.

You might say that my Christian faith has given me a perspective on life out here in the streets. I believe in Jesus Christ. My parents, before they died, were regular church-going Christians. They took my two brothers and me to church every week, and we got a solid spiritual foundation. My whole family was wiped out in a car accident in the mountains of New York. It was the first family vacation in a long time. My youngest brother was home from West Point, and my older brother was on summer break from graduate school. They were all killed in a head-on collision in upstate New York. They were the only family I had besides my church family.

After their deaths I felt estranged from everyone. The church no longer seemed to fill my needs, but I've always believed in Jesus Christ, in the power of his words and witness. Two things about Jesus have helped me survive. First, Jesus himself was a homeless person. Second, Jesus was also among the unemployed.

These two thoughts give me much comfort because they tell me that even God herself took on the plight and condition of the homeless and unemployed, but somehow managed to overcome its negative affects. That's why when that brother handed me that flyer offering hope because Jesus was among the unemployed, I felt God was speaking directly to me, helping me to make a way out of no way!

If Jesus was homeless and jobless, he knows how it feels to be wandering these streets. If Jesus came back today, he'd be right out here with me and other have-nots looking for a place to lay his head. Even Jesus wouldn't have a place to stay if he came back right now!

Now, God is saying a whole lot in that idea. God could have easily come back in a real comfortable situation. She could have had all the luxuries and creature comforts she wanted. But no, she did not come with all those things. She came as one of the least of these, the downtrodden and outcast of society.

These thoughts give me much relief and comfort because I know that God can still make a way out of no way. The very thing that gets me down is the same thing that God uses to pick me up. So I know that my homeless condition, however bad it might get sometimes, will be the very thing that saves me spiritually.

The rest of society gives its pitiful explanations of the wretchedness of homelessness—how bad it is and what a shame it is to have homeless people in the richest nation on earth. What the society does not see is how the homeless develop skills for survival with only the scarcest resources. The larger society does not see how the condition that it thinks is a big negative can turn out to be a real positive for some people. Notice I said *some* people. Not everybody is as analytical about this as I am. Everyone faced with such cruel choices in life can't develop a viewpoint that will help them become optimistic in the midst of extreme poverty and hopelessness. Perhaps I represent an exception to the rule rather than the rule itself, because lots of people are hopeless as well as homeless.

But if homelessness means having to survive on the barest resources, then the entire society is headed towards homelessness, because one of the biggest problems facing America is how to live with a pie that is constantly shrinking.

Homeless people have already learned how to survive with nothing. Society could learn a lot from us about how to do this. The problem is the sickness and disease that usually catches up with us and kills us. Because so much time is spent outside, I get a lot of colds. It's the disease which results from the *dis-ease* that finally kills us all. These are the things which constantly tear at the spirit and finally take us under. But if America ever wanted to learn how to make radical adjustments to its current problems, it could talk to homeless people to get an idea of how to adapt to such change. The very condition that society despises and detests is the same condition which might save it from complete destruction.

The meaning of Jesus' life is very clear to me. God made sense out of a senseless situation. God specializes in making a way out of no way and turning negatives into positives. Jesus' homelessness and unemployment give us clues as to how to have a home and how to have value in the eyes of a society that says that you are nothing unless you have a home and a job.

Jesus changed all of that. He said that you don't have to live in a house to have a home and you can still be a person of worth and value if you have the capacity to make a way out of no way. This is our greatest plus as a human race: the ability to make something better for ourselves and others.

So while other people are looking down on me, each day I find ways to look up, because I know that this situation will change for the better sooner or later, and I can take what I've learned out here to make life better for somebody else. The thing which brings us down can be the thing which builds us up and teaches us some of life's most important and valuable lessons.

What gives me hope is that I have not accepted homelessness as a permanent state of mind and existence. My mind is not homeless. My spirit is not homeless. Homelessness does not mean hopelessness. Homelessness describes my physical state of being. It does not define my permanent condition as a person of worth and value in my eyes and God's eyes.

That's the problem with this society. Too often the *description* of a condition becomes the grounds for the *definition* of the whole person. Jesus was homeless. That's a description of his social condition. It's not a definition of his spirituality, his worth as an instrument of God. I refuse to allow my physical condition to define my total worth as a person.

The problem comes when we buy into the definitions handed down to us by others. Homeless people have spirituality, intelligence, creativity, and other traits which make them people of worth. It's the social condition that's the problem—the fact that we have no permanent, acceptable place to lay our heads at night. The social condition is not the only means for defining the worth of individuals. It is not until the spiritual condition matches the social situation that we can say that one is truly homeless.

Most people have homes and cars and jobs. But they are truly homeless because they have a restless spirit that accepts their social description as a basis for defining their self-worth and potential. These people are more homeless than those who are physically so. Their entire lives revolve around the idea of getting, having, and spending. Their spirituality and their sensuality are all determined by their social status and situation.

You'd be amazed at the intelligence of some of the homeless people that society has defined as ignorant, unintelligent, and lazy. The social condition of these people has caused society to define their spirit and character as worthless. But if you engage any number of them in meaningful conversation, you'll discover that under the homeless surface lies a person of character and worth, someone who is not as shiftless, stupid, and irresponsible as society thinks.

There is a homeless brother named Rasputink. He never went to college but is a brilliant person. He has a profound philosophy of life. He can discuss any subject with any person. But society will never know the extent of his gifts because it allows the label of homelessness to define his whole being and potential. Some people work very hard to go beyond such definitions and labels, and Rasputink is a supreme example.

There's another lady named Marva. She has a master's degree in computer science. She walks the streets every day. In fact, she might walk in here at any minute. She is one of the throwaways of this society. She is a gifted person and extremely bright. But no one will ever know the potential of this lady because she is without a home.

In hearing about such people, especially the college-trained homeless, people recoil in horror. Immediately they think that there must be something deranged about such people. How could someone have a Master's degree and be homeless? What's wrong with her? She must have psychological problems. She's a freak of nature. Immediately the road blocks to sympathy are set up because society says no one in their right mind could be college educated and homeless! That's the way this society thinks.

Everybody asks what's wrong with Marva, but no one asks what's wrong with a society that throws away a person of her caliber and intelligence. You'd be surprised at how people out here who have all the ingredients of success have been devalued as human beings because of the social description of their plight.

That's why God makes a way out of no way. People like Marva and Rasputink are the very ones who could lead America back home to those values which view all people, regardless of their station or status, as worthy. It is this perspective that made America great in the first place. The least of these becomes the first of these.

I firmly believe that God is making an important statement through people like us. The rest of society needs to wake up and take a long, hard look at itself. God is constantly showing a way out of this mess, but no one seems to care or listen. The path least traveled, the rockiest, most terrible, dangerous, and torturous path is the "no way" through which God clears a path for us to follow. Often this path is the one most people don't want to travel, so God appoints others to lead the rest of society down that path. And that path is the very one which leads to sanity, order, and prosperity in society.

Homeless people, believe it or not, are leading the way down a path ordinary people don't want to follow because it's too painful. But if more people took a closer look at both the homeless people and the road they are traveling, they would learn more about how God is truly a way-maker and uses social outcasts to blaze new trails. A way out of no way becomes *the way* for God to make her purposes and plans known to the rest of creation. God is always making a way out of no way. I thank God for that!

Commentary

The idea of God making a way out of no way is an important construct of indigenous black theology and black spirituality. The least of these, the despised, rejected, alienated, and repudiated, have always found a path which has helped sustain their sanity in the midst of insane circumstances. This aspect of the Christian faith has been one of the central organizing themes of black Christianity. God invariably provides the coping resources and mechanisms for transcending the perils and plight of social contradictions. God is always revealing new ways of helping people and society fathom and transcend the constraints of their human condition. This often means choosing people to assume an unpopular path or lifestyle, which, with closer and more serious scrutiny, could provide answers to some of society's most plaguing maladies. The path that no one wants to travel becomes the very path that could reveal information which leads to a way out of the condition itself.

The paradox is that the larger culture often fails to recognize those "problem" people as reputable sources of learning and knowledge. After all, the people themselves are a large part of the problem. How could they provide answers to problems which they themselves personify? Society's estimation of their worth as a valuable source of problem-solving is viewed in terms of their capacity to eradicate their own condition. Failure to meliorate their own poverty constitutes grounds for the subordination of these individuals as *personna non grata*. The social definitions have thereby shaped the individual's capacities for self-worth. If the homeless are part of the problem, how could they be part of the solution? What valuable information could they disclose which would help eliminate their plight? If they had something of value, they wouldn't be homeless in the first place.

Indigenous black theology affirms that it is precisely under such conditions that God is at work to bring change amid order and order amid change. God continually chooses the path of the outsider, the path of the despised and rejected, as the means of obliterating their extraneous condition and dubious status. African American spirituality in general and indigenous black theology in particular have always declared the autonomy of God in choosing and revealing paths and sources of radical transformation through people who have been maligned as the primary cause of those problems. Jesus is one example. The path God chooses is often inimical to the conventional wisdom of society. The people God chooses to provide answers are viewed by the larger society as part of the problem itself. How can homelessness be eliminated? Talk to the homeless! They might provide valuable information as to how to address these issues societally.

God making a way out of no way means that God always provides answers to life's most bewitching enigmas and that answers can be found in the very sources that society has most devalued and maligned as untenable.

When our backs are against the wall and there seems to be no recourse or way out of such circumstances, perhaps *we* are the problem because of our failure to look beyond our own walls. We have so constricted our own parameters of thought that we cannot escape the psychological and spiritual restraints binding us.

In facing the dilemmas and racial quandaries of American society, African Americans have embraced a God who creatively provides a way out of such maddening and crippling circumstances. This God is one of hope and ingenuity, a God who always has the final word about the fate of the people. Where the social order and its dominators have failed to provide meaningful alternatives to the degenerative malaise impeding the fulfillment and self-realization of African Americans, God discloses the new way that answers all that troubles and bemuses the people of God.

Abraisha's firm belief in God's capacity to rescue the perishing is a testament to her optimism and faith. Such beliefs have always been a foundation of African American indigenous spirituality. Black people must believe that God is ultimately in charge of the universe and that she will provide meaningful options to the dead-end alternatives of a racist and myopic social order. God always reserves the right to do something new and different, to chart new thoroughfares of wisdom and interpretation which are counter to the status quo. The new thing God does always discomforts and perplexes the power brokers of society.

Belief in such a God is essential to the psychological and spiritual liberation of African Americans, for if one were to accept the present state as the final fate of black people, all hope would be forever cast to the winds. God is always making a way out of no way. We must utilize what God has given us to capitalize on our condition. We cannot allow the larger society to define and determine the value and worth of our condition, especially when such viewpoints prevent us from seeing our true potential. By providing a way out of no way, God continually exhorts us to that positive progressive change that is indispensable to human empowerment. When all else fails, God always provides a ram in the bush, a whole new way of seeing and acting that makes a way out of no way for us!

God Who's
Tighter Than
—Dick's Hatband—

Wardell Beasley has been an account executive for ten years at Sears and Joy Accounting Firm of New York City. He is an MBA graduate of Harvard Business School, and he took his B.S. degree from the University of Pennsylvania. A native of Tuscaloosa, Alabama, Wardell has a gift for gab and a penchant for humor that are reminiscent of African American folk traditions.

As a "lean and green teenager who didn't have a pot or a window to throw it out of," he was fired from his first job as a waiter in a Selma, Alabama restaurant for stealing cooked greens and cornbread from the owner's cache of food. Moreover, to deceitfully cover his tracks and to protect his own daily stash, he informed customers that the greens they were ordering had been contaminated by a pesticide spray of unknown origin and that eating them would cause chills, fever, and sudden death. This ploy lead to the first official greens scare of Dallas county and the subsequent termination of his employment. We are sitting in his meagerly appointed Brooklyn apartment, listening to John Lee Hooker's "Boom. Boom." Here is his story.

Wardell's Narrative

Man, there's about twenty million stories in the naked city, and I ain't one of 'em. I was born, bred, and fed in Tuscaloosa, Alabama. My daddy boogied when I was two, and my mama scrubbed the floors of white folks' houses to make a living. I'll never forget, man, how I went to visit her on the job, and I saw her on her hands and knees, fine-tuning them floors with a small toothbrush. Them floors were so clean you could have Sunday dinner right off of them without a plate. My mama was a good religious woman who loved the Lord. She died when I was twelve, and then I went to live with my Aunt Cussie in Selma.

That's a heck of a name for a woman, ain't it? After living with her for three days, I understood why they called her Cussie. She could cuss a negro out quicker than a slave pickin' cotton.

She could use the word "motha" eighteen different times in one sentence, and they would all have different meanings. Her husband say she got that name when she was a baby. Rumor has it that she cussed out the milkman when she was two years old. The first time I didn't clean up my room, she cussed me out. Mailman came, she'd cuss him out. If the butcher cut the wrong size of meat, she'd cuss him out. The only person she didn't cuss around was Reverend Braithwhite Bottoms. But one day she slipped, right there in church. Just as Deacon Fowler was launching into one of them around the world, Holy Ghost prayers—man, he could pray and pray long; negroes had better pack a lunch when Deacon Fowler prayed. When asked why he prayed so long, he jokingly said the scriptures say to pray without ceasing. "Danged Fowler," Deacon Jones said. "You confusing eternity with everlasting!"

Anyway, Fowler was praying, man, when Aunt Cussie jumped up and shouted, "Thank you, Jesus!" Now, some of the kids sitting behind her took to an experiment. Everybody knew Aunt Cussie would jump up with the Holy Ghost at eleven fifteen every Sunday morning. This time when she came back down she would be in for a surprise. Terdell and Junior Rollins planted two lumberyard tacks in her seat, and when she came down, she went right back up and shouted, "Oh sh—! Help me, Jesus!"

Man, we laughed so hard they almost had to close church. People were all in the floor rolling around laughing, 'cause when Aunt Cussie jumped up, her purse went one way, her bible went another way, and her hat shot straight up in the air and landed on the pew in front of her. Rev. Bottoms, who was five-two and three hundred fifty pounds, tried to ease sideways to the podium like a fleet-footed dancer to restore order because people had lost control with their laughter. They were in frenzied fits of uncontrollable jubilation. It was all the funnier seeing the sneak-thief look on Aunt Cussie's face. She had always played like she was so polite and courteous around the good Reverend, and now she was completely embarrassed by what had happened.

"We must have order in this service," said Reverend Bottoms in a low authoritative bellow. "Deacons, please restore order! This is the Lawd's house, and we must govern ourselves according to the statutes and regulations of our Lawd and Savior!"

When he said that in his slow, meticulous way, we laughed even harder. Reverend Bottoms was trying hard to be proper under conditions that had lost all propriety. Clearing this throat, he lost some of his decorum. "I said, ya'll need to *hush up* in here. This is the *Lawd's* house, and we must govern ourselves accordingly. The scriptures say when a fool speaks, even the wise pay penance by keeping watch. Now watch yourselves and pay attention to what I'm saying! Sister Wilson, what seems to be the problem?" he shouted in a holy tone of voice. Bewildered, embarrassed, and confused, she looked around and pulled out a tack still painfully piercing her behind.

"Somebody put a tack in my seat! Probably one of these heathen children," she shouted, turning and staring sternly at Terdell and Junior, who by now had stopped laughing. "One of these dat-gummed, dern-blasted kids put a tack in my seat, which ain't nothing but the devil," she yelled, wagging her finger in their faces. "I'm telling you, I've never been so disgusted and humiliated in my life. The devil is busy through the little chirun in the church! Lord have mercy! We's all going to hell!" she said, as if she were second-guessing herself about whether hell was a cuss word.

"Terdell did it," hollered Junior plaintively.

"You a story, you did it," retorted Terdell.

"You know you telling one," shouted Junior at the top of his voice.

"Terdell, I want to see you, Junior, and your mama after service in my office. I'll get to the bottom of this," said Pastor Bottoms, as they both hung their heads in shame.

Still embarrassed and crying, Aunt Cussie got up and stormed out of church amid the snickers and giggles of the parishioners. Life would never be the same after that. All the people in church gossiped about Aunt Cussie. The kids started calling her "Aunt Tackie."

Her husband, my uncle Cleavus, said that what had happened must have been a sign from God. "The way that woman cussed, God had to find a way to stop all that stuff," he said. "Didn't make no sense for the woman to be cussing people out Monday through Saturday and then sit in church on Sunday with that wide, toothy grin, pretending to be an angel." Aunt Cussie didn't cuss too much after that. She'd just cuss a negro out if he made her mad, but she didn't cuss to be cussing no more.

Terdell and Junior got into big trouble. Their daddy found out, and they got the daylights beat out of them. Things got real bad for them. Both boys got put on punishment for a year. They couldn't go outside. Couldn't go to the movies. They had to stay inside and could only go to school and church.

One day I was walking by their house and saw Terdell sitting in the window, playing with the window shade and looking real dumb and stupid.

"Hey, Terddie, come on out and play," I shouted laughingly.

"Man, you know I can't come out. It's tighter than Dick's hatband in here. My daddy and mama won't let me do nothing. If I fart, they send me to my room. If I look like I want to fart, they add another week to this life sentence," he said sorrowfully. "Man, I'm about to go crazy in this house. It's dead of summer. It's hotter than Hades in this house, and I can't go nowhere. If you read about me in the paper, you'll know I done gone stone crazy."

"What you mean, read about you in the paper?" I asked.

"You know, man, read in the headlines of the Times, "Terdell Rollins Kills Parents With Hacksaw. Parents' One Year Punishment Drove Him Crazy."

"Come on, man, it ain't that bad, is it?"

"Yeah, it's that bad. I told you it was tighter than Dick's hatband up in here. We can't do nothing. We got to get permission to breathe up in here. It's like my daddy done lost his mind, and my mama is barely speaking to us. I been having some real long talks with God, man, to let me off the hook. It's so tight up in here, I feel like calling the police, but my daddy's the warden and we're already in jail."

"I understand, man, but you boys shouldn't have put those tacks in Aunt Cussie's seat. Your daddy is just trying to make you think about what you did, that's all," I said.

"But how long am I supposed to think about this? Every time I think about what we did I just bust out laughing. Man, that was the funniest stuff, seeing Aunt Cussie jump straight up with her big behind self," he said. "But every time I think about how long I've got to stay inside, it ain't funny no more."

"Yeah, but you paying for it now, boy."

"You got that right, and paying like a big dog," he said, slightly amused.

That expression, "tighter than Dick's hatband," became a very popular slogan all around our neighborhood. Everybody used that phrase to describe a variety of situations and conditions. Even Reverend Bottoms used that phrase in sermons every now and then.

Once he did a sermon titled, "Tighter Than Dick's Hatband." I'll never forget it. It was about Daniel in the lion's den. How things got real tight for Daniel but God somehow loosened the grip Satan was trying to wrap around his life. God's freeing Daniel because of his faith was God's way of providing ease to Daniel's discomfort. "Tighter than Dick's hatband" became a phrase which signified the extremities of our human situation requiring God's miraculous intervention.

God is about discipline, about following certain rules and regulations. If we violate his rules, we pay a big price. That's when things get real tight. Even in the bible, from Adam and Eve to Elijah to Moses and Jesus, everyone was placed into predicaments that made things real tight for them, where there seemed to be no way out. Sometimes things got tight as a result of decisions they made, and that's how it is for us.

It got tight for Adam and Eve when they disobeyed and ate of the tree of knowledge. It got tight for Cain and Abel when they went to blows over who was their mama and daddy's favorite. It got tight for Moses when he was taking the Hebrews through the wilderness and when he killed that Egyptian soldier. It got tight for Elijah when Ahab and Jezebel put him on the run. And you know it got tight for Jesus when he was hanging on the cross. Some of his last words could have been, "My God, my God, why have things become so tight for me?"

God has a plan he wants us to follow. It's a carefully laid plan. When we violate or even unfaithfully follow his plan for our lives, we are thrown into tight situations which threaten to strangle the life out of us. It gets tight for everybody. The question is whether God will loosen the hold that our tight situations bind us in. We spend our entire lives trying to figure out how to get out of the tight fix.

God being tighter than Dick's hatband means that God has carefully laid plans for our lives that we are to follow; if we deviate from them, we pay the price. But the phrase also means that our relationship with God should be one of a tightness—intimacy, if you will—that is closer than no other.

Just like the hatband which sits snugly and tightly against the crown of a Dobbs or Stetson, our relationship with God should be the same—a relationship in which nothing can come between or separate us from God. The hatband is united with the hat very firmly. If the hatband comes loose, the crown loses its form and the hat no longer reflects the beauty of the maker.

Our relationship with God is the same way. Whenever we become separated from God by doing the wrong things, we lose our beauty and the things which make us good. We should all be striving to achieve a unity with God that no one can ever destroy. This is what God wants for us.

One thing that has saved black people in America is this tight relationship with God. God is our original homey. Were it not for our relationship with God, we would have gone crazy as a people a long time ago. There is no way we could keep our sanity in this crazy place without believing in some higher power that we know is looking out for us.

Close friends are real tight, and that's what our relationship with God should be like. Just like nothing can ever come between close friends, nothing should ever come between ourselves and God.

This lesson was driven home to me when I first went to U Penn and got my first gig with an accounting firm. All the white boys were jockeying and profiling for positions with the boss, and I just kept my cool through it all. They were cutting each other's throats and not even waiting for the blood to dry. It was awful. One day this white boy named John, who was one of the main instigators of the power grab, confronted me at the pop machine about why I was so cool and laid back about everything. "You black guys are always so cool. Why do you stand around and hold your crotch? It is because you're trying to be cool?" he demanded sarcastically.

I felt insulted and outraged. First, I don't stand around and hold my crotch. Second, what is he doing looking at my crotch? Third, why am I so important to him that he wants to call me out like this?

I asked him what his problem was, why he felt he needed to dis me in this manner. "You got a problem?" I demanded. "Why are you white boys always interested in what black men are doing with their crotches? It's probably because you got a crotch problem yourself, don't you think?" I said forcefully. He turned and walked away, embarrassed. Now, what gave him the license to come at me this way? White folks always think they have a license to insult and disgrace us whenever they get a liking. This insecurity is most manifest with white men!

I always remember my mama saying, "Boy, whatever you do and wherever you go, don't ever let people get between you and your God, especially white folks. Keep God close, and you'll never be sorry." From then on I decided to have a relationship with God that was tighter than Dick's hatband. I was determined not to allow people to ruffle my feathers and veer me off course to destroy me. As a black man in a white, racist society, this is always a problem. White folks and handkerchief-head colored folks are always trying to bring you down, trying to make you get outside and beside yourself. If people can make you lose yourself, they win. But if you have a relationship with God and know who you are and don't let anybody come between you and him, you can have control and power over your life. So long as white folks can't come between us and God, they will never be fully able to control us or have absolute power over black people in America. In fact, I have a saying: "The closer your relationship with God, the stronger you are able to fend off your adversaries."

Some people don't believe this, but I believe that God wants us to have that kind of relationship with him, where nothing can come between us and nothing can stand in the way of us making the right choices and decisions.

I remember one of my professors at U Penn tried to test me to see what I was made of. I wrote a fabulous paper. I spent long hours writing and rewriting it and knew I had done an outstanding job. Got a C grade for the paper. Totally made me mad! When the professor passed out the papers in class, he knew I was miffed when I got mine and saw the grade. I couldn't believe I got a C when I deserved an A. He confronted me after class.

"Sorry about the grade," he said. "You could have done better."

Knowing what he was up to, I said, "Yes, that's right, Professor. I could have done better. This means I will have to work harder."

He expected me to cuss him out and call him all kind of names, but I didn't. After that he had a new respect for me. He appointed me a special fellow to work on a project with him. It was all in my response. No more C papers either. He had some humanity, but my close relationship with God made the difference. I am determined not to allow others to come between me and the Lord by making me do something I might regret later. A relationship with God that's tighter than Dick's hatband should be what we all are striving for. There is no greater satisfaction in life than knowing you are close to God and God is close to you and nothing can come between you.

People are always trying to figure you out and push your buttons. There's something in human nature that enjoys seeing and making other people cut the fool. If people can make you respond to things according to their terms, they will always have power over you. You will always be a slave. That's one problem with us. We let too many people have a say about our behavior and our destiny. We allow too many people to tell us what to do, how to act, when and what to think. We are always begging and blaming white folks for stuff because we've given them too much power in our lives. If we have a problem, we go to them for answers. Never mind that they are a big part of the problem. But when you look at it, the real problem is us because we give them too much power and control over us. If we started looking to ourselves to solve our own problems, we would be much further along. You would think by now that after all these years, we would have learned the lessons of history.

It all begins with our self-concept and our understanding of who God is and our striving to have a relationship with God that's tighter than Dick's hatband. If we have the right relationship with God and work to keep tight with God, other people would not pose as many problems for us. If we had tighter relationships with God, we would know what to do, how to act, and what to think, because through our conversations with God, he would be telling us what to do. By being tight with God, we are open to what God wants for our lives. If we don't have a tight relationship, then we become open prey to any whim or idea that people use to keep an edge over us.

Think about it. Think about how people are always trying to manipulate each other for power. It happens in every area of life. Somebody's always trying to figure us out, trying to push our buttons so we can act a fool. Then our acting the fool confirms all the crazy stuff they believe about us in the first place. When we refuse to be manipulated, refuse to have our buttons pushed, then we become a source of confusion. They *really* try to figure us out then. But as long as we are bowing, scraping and acting like white folks want us to act, they'll think they have control over us.

I have a close relationship with God. I don't laugh when things ain't funny. I don't scratch if I don't have no itch. I don't apologize for not laughing, and I don't apologize for not scratching.

I remember a black co-worker, Harlan Harmonds, also a Harvard MBA graduate, came to me after a conference meeting with all the executive staff. He was really worried and nervous about how I seemed to isolate myself from other people. In other words, he would see me in the lunch room sitting by myself or with other black co-workers. Seldom do I sit with people who give bad vibes, black or white. Anyway, he asked me one day, "Wardell, why don't you ever sit with whites? Some of them have been carping about how all the blacks always sit together and eat lunch and that you never sit with them."

I almost lost my cool. "Why is it always a problem when we sit with each other? Why do we always have to justify and apologize to white folks when more than two or three of us are gathered? They can sit in their little groups and it's okay. But the minute we get together, there's a problem. There's a conspiracy. I sit with who I want to sit with, and it ain't nobody's business who I sit with. I don't ever see any of them breaking their necks to sit with us. Why should we be breaking our necks to sit with them? Why does this have to be a problem, and why you bringing me this jive, anyway?" I asked furiously.

"Well, it was a concern...."

"Whose concern?" I broke in abruptly. "Whose concern is it? It ain't my concern! Why should it be your concern or their concern? I sit with whom I choose. If my white colleagues and I decide to sit down and have lunch together, we do it! But why do I have to be under some mandate to always act in ways that please white folks and make them comfortable? If they got a problem with who I sit with, tell them to talk with me about it personally instead of sending you as their emissary!"

From that day on, the brother was afraid of me. He never sat with us or fraternized with the blacks because he was afraid and ashamed. White folks had made him feel guilty about hanging with his own kind. He would never be a free man in my opinion because he was too worried about what other folks thought about him. If he wasn't free enough to sit with his own kind in the cafeteria, how could he be free in other more important areas of his life? He is good brother with a lot of gifts. He just ain't free.

This typifies part of our problem. We don't trust God enough to be ourselves. Because of our insecurities, we always have to be checking with other folks to get permission to behave in certain ways. It's like being on the plantation, only now we have taken these pathologies into the plant.

Having a relationship with God that's tighter than Dick's hatband means you know that God has your back covered. You trust and rely upon God absolutely. You are not afraid of other people, and you are not afraid of being who God has called you to be. In other words, you live fearlessly. You live with confidence, not arrogance. You are secure in yourself and are satisfied with what God has created you to be—a man, with thoughts and aspirations like other men! I will never give another man, black or white, the keys to my kingdom or my manhood. I don't care how much power they think they have. So long as I have a tight relationship with God, no man can take that away. I don't care what he's got in his arsenal or in his bag of psychological tricks, I'm going to keep on being who I am and not what he wants me to be in order to make himself feel more secure. I do my work. I am polite to people. I treat other people, black or white, with respect when I am given respect. But I don't respect nobody who don't respect me, and I don't go out of my way to make no white or colored folks feel good for no reason, especially when they want me to lessen my power profile to make them feel better. I get sick and tired of people always putting you on the defensive and making black people feel guilty about assuming some semblance of normalcy in life. I made up my mind a long time ago that I wasn't going to spend the rest of my life shuffling and cow-towing to folks just to make them feel better. The same time and energy we spend on doing such crazy things could be used to better our condition in this country.

But again, in my mind, it all goes back to that relationship with God. If you're tight with God and are determined to not let anyone destroy your confidence in him and in yourself, especially for doing the right thing, you can be a free person. You can live your life with dignity. But if you don't have that relationship, who's going to back you when you take a stand against the foolishness of this world? When people turn their backs on you, you need a backup you can rely on that will give you strength and confidence. Your relationship with God determines how you perceive yourself and the world around you, how you respond to the things of this life which make or break you. You see, it's the little things that happen on a day-to-day basis that break us down. We always talk about how kids are killing kids and how the white man is oppressing us and we can't break free. This is true, but you know what really kills us? Narrow mindedness, fear, envy, jealousy, and all those other human feelings which bind and oppress and kill our spirits and our desire to do more for ourselves.

I've known many a teacher who has killed the spirit of a potentially good student by saying things to that student to destroy his confidence and desire to learn. The student experiences a slow and agonizing death of his will to learn and his desire to better himself because the very people he has been taught to respect tear him down. This is worse than any political oppression of any governing despot. We always think of the big things which oppress, repress, and destroy people—Stalin's purges, the massacres of the Pol Pot regime in Cambodia, and atrocities committed in other places. But nothing is worse than those oppressions experienced on a daily basis that are performed under the guise of legitimacy, particularly by those whose vocation is to inspire confidence and instill a desire to better oneself.

The angry parent who continually tells the child she or he will never amount to anything is equally deadly, especially when his or her diatribes take away the child's self-confidence. These things wound the soul and maim the spirit of that child worse than anything else. Once people take away your ability to believe in yourself, they have taken the keys to your kingdom. The things we do to each other as part of the subtleties of life's daily experiences often devastate us more that what other people do to us.

That's why our relationship with God is the most important thing for us. It's something other people can't touch. It is the pivotal center of our self-identity and self-confidence. When other people are coming at me all wrong, I fall back on God to get me right. Our relationship with God is the one thing that white folks have never been able to touch. If we keep that intimacy, we keep our power and self-confidence as a people. Nothing baffles people more than trying to figure out what makes us tick. I learned a long time ago that if you keep tight with God, you keep your sanity, your power, and your personal dignity amid the cruelty and chaos of this world. That's the key to everything—our well being, our freedom, our knowledge, and our destiny: God, what we think about God, how we feel about God, and what we believe that God is calling us to do in a world that's always trying to mold us for its own manipulative and destructive purposes.

Tighter than Dick's hatband. That's what God is with me. It is the key to our survival, our uplift, and our perseverance as a people. It is the key to history, self-dignity, self-empowerment, and self-transformation. If we keep that relationship with God tight as a hatband around the crown of a hat, we will always be able to say, like Sade, "Nothing can come between us," and like M.C. Hammer, "You Can't Touch This!"

Commentary

The most important thing to Wardell Beasley is his relationship with God. More than any other entity in his life, God is the supreme source of personal identity and empowerment. In a world that continually attempts to describe, define, and redefine the human person, the God-self relationship provides a steady source of confidence, hope, and renewal amid the chaos of a racist society. A close relationship with God means that the individual's power center cannot be manipulated by outside forces. Only the individual can determine his or her own destiny in accordance with the will of God, and this is mediated through a sustained personal relationship with God.

The problem is that too many people are distracted by other forces and realities which determine their identity. Human consciousness and will are shaped by myriad social and political realities which often undermine the individual's sense of purpose. This has been the problem in the history of African Americans. White people have always reserved the right to describe and define the being, value, and worth of black people. Such descriptions and definitions have always reinforced the disparity of existing power structures. Because black people have always been predominantly defined in terms of their problems or recognized as the big problem of American society, the interpretations become self-fulfilling prophecies. So long as whites define blacks as the problem, they can justify the existence of those forces of psychological and physical repression which create and perpetuate social disparity and oppression. For Wardell and others, however repressive and oppressive the larger society becomes, it can never dictate the bases by which individuals choose to live out the terms of their existence. Once the larger society has the power to define life's meaning and purpose, the individual is no longer free. Freedom not only issues from the political and social citadels of the society, but from the individual's desire to live life on his own terms.

An intimate and personal relationship with God becomes the basis of self-determination. Man created society, but man did not create God. The personal relationship with God is the individual's last refuge of personal autonomy and freedom. While society may determine to some extent the material conditions of the oppressed, it can never fully determine the spiritual and relational conditions that inspire personal freedom. The oppressed say, "You can take everything away, but you can't take away my relationship with God. Once you take that away, I am no longer free. A personal relationship with God is the paramount source of self-identity, pride, imagination, and creativity. Without these things, I am not a free person."

"Tighter than Dick's hatband" is a cultural expression of black people that signifies a state of togetherness with a particular thing. The notion of God being the intimate source of personal identity largely emanates from the archives of African American life and culture. All people should be striving for an intimacy with God that cannot be severed by social, political, or racial realities. This closeness is what has enabled black people to survive the cruelties of the American experience. Without a relationship of absolute trust and reliance on God, more blacks would have succumbed to the terrible rounds of persecution and discrimination lived from day to day.

Moreover, the way we conceptualize, interpret, and relate to God through personal experience is highly different from the ways of white folks. Our relationship with God is therefore the fundamental, indispensable factor differentiating our quality of life and our capacity to live with dignity while maintaining our sanity amid the inanities of the American experience.

What allows the black person to maintain his personal cohesion and well-being in the throes of American culture and society? His relationship with God. What has enabled black people to survive the unwarranted tumult and tragedies heaped upon them through the American experience? Their intimate relationship with God. It is because of black people's relationship with God that they have surmounted the incredible difficulties of the American experience.

Wardell and other black people like him have come to their theologies in the vortex of day-to-day experience. They have learned that by keeping God at the center of their lives they will always have the spiritual leverage which empowers genuine self-determination.

Indigenous black theology affirms the importance of spiritual and relational intimacy with God. Knowing, trusting, and relying on God is essential to maintaining personal and spiritual autonomy. A hallmark of indigenous thought is that there is a realm of the God-human relationship that cannot be shaped or influenced by others. It is endemic to that individual. It is sacred and personal, an area of being and existence that is off-limits to everyone.

The intimate relationship with God is the one thing that African Americans have that white people cannot touch. Black culture is the one area of black existence that preserves the uniqueness and creative character of African American life. The God of the personal experience, with whom black people have a very close and contiguous relationship, provides the foundation for all notions of personal and collective freedom.

Indigenous black theology affirms both the sanctity and value of this intimate spiritual relationship. It is the foundation of black life and being and the compelling force of creative change in the lives of African Americans. The mind of God is a mind of its own, and only those having a close relationship with God can be in intimate contact with God's revealed purposes for their lives. The more black people allow others to define and shape this relationship with God, the more plausible the loss of freedom, creativity, and spontaneity becomes, all of which are kingpins of African American life and culture. Once the individual loses the intimate God relationship, they invariably lose the self-concept which is critical in the formation of black consciousness and identity.

An important aspect of indigenous thought is maintaining the freedom of personal autonomy, which means the power to choose the terms, conditions, nature, and trajectory of personal existence in American society. The central freedom of indigenous thought thus culminates in the freedom to create and live out one's existence in accordance with the creativity and dictates of personal choice. Freedom is preserved in the ability to fashion life according to the realities of everyday black experience in America. Without this freedom, the unique identity and the formative factors of cultural expression are obscured by the determinants and ethos of the larger culture.

All forms of indigenous thought, from Native American to African American, affirm the right of indigenous persons to develop belief systems and mythos which reflect their unique identity and freedom to create life and culture in accordance with the trajectories of those belief systems.

Indigenous black theology values the personal, intimate relationship with God as the source of personal identity and empowerment and the wellspring and fount of unique creative and cultural expressions. As stated earlier, the larger society may influence the development, formation, and impact of material conditions, but it can never impact the spiritual conditions which influence the formation and empowerment of the positive, proactive black self.

God of What Goes Around —Comes Around—

Beulah Jeanette Draper is a sixty-six-year-old black woman born and raised in Tallahassee, Florida. She is married and has four children and thirteen grandchildren. A devoutly religious woman, she is the spiritual matriarch of her community and is known to have great healing powers.

A staunch Christian and activist in the struggle for civil and human rights, she was instrumental in mobilizing black people to freedom in Florida during the civil rights era. She marched with Dr. King throughout the South, and her tireless efforts have been lauded throughout the black community. Possessing only an eighth-grade education, she is extremely learned, well-read, and conversant on many subjects. As a child of the South, she has experienced her share of racial injustice. In considering all the indignities black people have suffered, she believes that those who have inflicted them will be repaid for their sins. No one escapes the impending judgment of his own actions. God rectifies such situations through a variety of human circumstances. The Lord is God of "what goes around comes around." Here is her story.

Beulah's Narrative

My great-grandfather was a medicine man from Nigeria. I used to hear the old folks talk about his powers, how he healed people and gave them herbs and medicines to make them well. It's funny how the white people changed our medicine men into witch doctors. They weren't witch doctors. There was nothing sorcerous or bewitching about them. Whenever white folks don't understand our culture, they place these belittling and degrading labels on it. My great-grandfather was a medicine man who studied natural medicine as it was practiced by the Yoruba tribe. I come from a long line of medicine people who specialized in healing other people.

Long ago, I remember my ancestors telling me stories of the motherland, how the great spirits grieved when we came to this land and how the over-spirit did not grieve long because it knew the importance we would have in settling the new land and in leading the white man back to his own humanity. Despite the inhumane things done to us in slavery and beyond, it would be our patience, long suffering, and good will that would show our oppressors the way back to their own sense of the sacred.

We could have easily ended slavery a long time ago. All the cooks could have taken care of that. All they had to do was poison their masters, and it would have all been over. I remember reading where many people of the Roman aristocracy, during the heyday of the great Roman empire, went insane and lost their minds. It was later discovered that their Greek slaves, whom they treated cruelly, took to cooking their food in lead pots. What was thought to be insanity was really lead poisoning. Some speculate that it was really the Greek cooks who brought the empire down to its knees and not the invading German barbarians.

The point is we could have ended slavery very easily, but our humanity, our sense of the sacred, our relationship with the God of "what goes around comes around" stopped us from killing our white masters, and that's the honest-to-God truth.

Our belief in this God is what has sustained us through the years. There is no way we could have survived the terrible nightmares of slavery without believing that God would one day serve justice and reverse all wrong done to us. Black people have always had confidence that white folks would get theirs for the things they did to us. This God of justice is the one who holds the scales and the forces that balance all nature. We have believed in this ever since our days in the Motherland. We have always known that what goes around always comes around. This is true on every level of life. There is virtually no level of life where the pendulum of justice does not swing back once it's tilted and swayed in the opposite direction.

Since the beginning of my time on this earth, I have always found this to be true. I remember hearing tales, some of them very tall, about how justice always triumphed on the side of right and truth. God is always on the side of right and truth, straightening everything that has been made crooked by the deeds of evil and corrupt men.

I have seen and experienced this principle over and over again. For example, I remember when my uncle Claudell, who was a strong black man who had a habit of talking back to white folks who were out of order, got into an argument at the town store over the cost of a bill. The owner of the store was a man named Murchison.

Mr. Murchison had a habit of padding the bills of black people. It was unwritten law that he would let you have groceries and other things on credit, but when you went in to pay the monthly bill, it would always be much more than what the groceries originally cost you. If you had accumulated twenty-five dollars worth of debt, you could rest assured that your bill would be forty dollars when it came time to pay.

Mr. Murchison called it his nigger tax. Whatever cost white folks one thing would cost us double. Everybody in town knew this was how he operated. We just went along with it because we couldn't do no better.

One day uncle Claudell went in to pay his bill of thirty-five dollars. But when he got the bill, he saw that it was for seventy-five dollars. "How is my bill seventy-five dollars when I only spent thirty five? Everybody knows about your black tax, but this is highway robbery! I got the receipts right here to show how much I should pay!" he shouted, pulling the receipts out of his tattered brown wallet in his back pants pocket. "You got to be out of your mind if you think I'm gonna pay this!" screamed Claudell, waving his fist in the air.

"Now just hold on here, Boy!" shouted Murchison, grabbing his shotgun and running from behind the counter all red-faced. "I'm tired of you niggers coming in here talking about the bill is wrong. The bill is right. Half of you can't count anyway, and I know you ain't calling me no liar," he said, hoisting the shotgun to his shoulder and pointing it at Uncle Claudell. "I got a mind to blow your darned head off right here and now, Boy, for making me a liar on my own property. Now, you know that white folks don't take too kindly to you niggers having any kind of mind in the first place," he said disdainfully while cocking the trigger.

"I say this bill ain't right, and you know it ain't right! I ain't spent no seventy-five dollars in here! I ain't got seventy-five dollars to spend, and I know I ain't spent that kind of money in this here store! Do I look like some back-woods nigger fool to you, Murchison? Do I look like a nigger with a wooden head? Do you think I done lost my mind, that I can't read? That I can't think and can't count? Naw, you been ripping me off for years, and I'm sick and tired of you running me down like this. It ain't right! God don't like it, and you gonna get yours! I ain't paying it this time! I ain't paying it! Last month my bill was only twenty-five dollars, and when I come to pay, it jumps to thirty-five! I didn't say nothing. I went along with it. The month before that my bill was sixteen dollars and sixty-seven cents. I get the bill and it's twenty-eight dollars! This month my bill is thirty-five dollars and you gonna charge me seventy-five dollars? I'm not paying no seventy-five dollars! You got to be plum out of your mind if you think I'm going to keep doing this injustice to myself."

"You'll pay it if I say you'll pay it! You calling me a liar, Boy? What makes you think I'd go through the trouble of trying to cheat you?" asked Murchison.

"I'm not paying it! I'll pay what I owe and that's it. Case closed!" Claudell boomed.

"I said you'll pay it out of your pocket, or you'll pay with your life," screamed Murchison. His hands were jittery, and his left eye was twitching uncontrollably.

"Oh, what, you threatening me now? You think I'm scared of you? You think I'm afraid of you? Go ahead and pull the trigger," said Claudell with a crazed look in his eye. "You white folks been killing black folks for years. You think I'm afraid to die, that I'm afraid to look you in your eye and call you a liar? Go ahead and pull the trigger, but don't think you won't pay! Don't think you won't have hell to pay," he said, walking towards Murchison and clinching his fist.

"You take another step forward, and I'll splatter your brains all over this store. You take one more step and they'll be scraping you up from in here! I'm warning you, Boy, one more step and it's eternity for you!" said Murchison, his voice rising to a high shrill.

At that point Uncle Claudell, who was six foot six, three hundred forty pounds, began laughing at old man Murchison, mocking him and calling him all kinds of spineless white fools. It's like he just didn't care. He had always been a fearless man, and now he had pulled out all the stops. Here was a southern white store owner holding a double-barreled shotgun on this big black man, threatening to kill him, and the black man was laughing in his face. This kind of thing was unheard of in the South in the 1940s, black folks defying white folks, talking back, and daring them to do something crazy.

Black people simply bowed to white folks and said "yes, sir" and "no, ma'am." But here was a man who stood his ground and dared Murchison to pull the trigger. Claudell had drawn the line. He had had enough. He would no longer allow the white man to denigrate and exploit him in such a humiliating manner.

"If you gonna shoot, shoot!" shouted Claudell. "You still won't get your money! You still won't get paid," he said, laughing. "Pull the trigger! Murch, pull the trigger! You crackers are all alike. You think you can do whatever you want to black people. We been taking crap off you for years, and we ain't taking it no more! What goes around comes around, and now it's time for you to get what's coming to you. So go ahead, pull the trigger and kill this here nigger!" he said sarcastically.

At that moment, Murchison fired a blast of double O buckshot straight into Uncle Claudell's face, making good on his promise to splatter his brains all over his country store. It was a horrible thing. It was a terrible sight! Another black life wasted for no reason at all. A life wasted because of racial hatred! Murchison was wrong. Uncle Claudell refused to comply with being ripped off and decided he wasn't going to pay for a bill that was a four hundred percent overcharge.

What made matters worse is that Murchison lied about what had happened. He said that Claudell came at him with a knife because he didn't want to pay his grocery bill. They ruled it self-defense, and he got off scott-free.

The whole thing was a case of white man's justice from start to finish. They didn't care that a family had lost a loved one. To them it was just another dead nigger buried in Oak Lawn cemetery and one less "monkey" to worry about in a small southern town.

Murchison went on overcharging black people on their grocery bills, but payday finally came for him for what he did to Uncle Claudell. Uncle Claudell had a twin brother, Cleophus, who had moved to New York in search of a better life. When Uncle Cleophus found out about what happened to his brother, he became very angry. Nobody really knew what Cleophus did in New York. We just knew he was doing very well because he would send big money home on a regular basis. He sent my mother, his baby sister, money all the time.

One day Cleophus showed up with three of his men. They were really mean-looking fellows. They never smiled. They wore dark sunglasses and trench coats and went everywhere he went. He kept wanting to hear about how his twin brother died. We told him the story so much that it got on our nerves. If it hadn't been for Thomas Thomas, who saw and overheard everything from the street, we would never have known what really happened in Murchison's store that fateful day.

Anyway, we kept rehashing the details of what had happened. Finally Cleophus decided to go to the store himself. "I think I'll go down to that little store and open myself a grocery account," he said. Although Cleophus and Claudell were twins, they looked nothing alike, except that they both had the same big, burly stature. Other than that, Murchison would have no clue that they were related.

Cleophus put on a pair of Claudell's overalls and an old Florida Seminoles cap and went down to the store. He was determined to get to the bottom of what really happened to Claudell.

"I hear ya'll offer credit in here," he said, tipping his hat and walking in with his wide, toothy grin.

"Sure do, for boys like yourself," said Murchison patronizingly. "Long as you can prove you got a J.O.B., you can get yourself some credit," he said almost laughingly. "Where you from?"

"Where I'm from ain't important. What the terms you offering?" asked Cleophus.

"Terms?" repeated Murchison, somewhat perplexed that such a statement would come from a negro.

"Yeah, holmes, terms. You know what *terms* are don't you? You know, *financing*? Finance charges for the *credit* you offer? Every business has *terms*. You ain't giving credit for *free* is you, man?"

"Well, no," said Murchison, scratching his big bald head.

"So what's the terms, man? You ain't giving something for nothing, is you? You couldn't run a big pretty store like this and not charge people for the credit you give them. I look like some kind of fool to you? I'm smarter than that. So what's the terms?" demanded Cleophus impatiently.

"It varies."

"What you mean, varies?"

"You know. It varies from day to day, depending upon a combination of factors," said Murchison nervously.

"What are the factors? The prime rate? Standard bank interest rates? Federal Reserve calculation? Stock market fluctuations? Dow Jones? Nikkei? Or what?"

"Basically, they're my terms! I decide what the rates will be depending upon a variety of factors. How long I've known you. How well you pay your bills. Your attitude, disposition, and even sometimes how I feel on any given day," he said belligerently, passing Cleophus a credit application.

"Fine, sign me up," said Cleophus, cheerfully filling out the form.

After the first week Cleophus incurred thirty-eight dollars in debt and was charged the exact amount. The next week he charged forty-nine dollars and was not penalized a penny more. The third week, however, he charged fifty-four dollars in groceries, and when he went to pay the bill, he received the shock of his life. The bill totaled ninety-six dollars in charges, most of which he could not decipher because they were written in a deliberately obscure script on a worn brown paper bag. The tension between Murchison and Uncle Cleophus had been escalating for weeks. Many townsfolk said that Murchison thought Cleophus was an uppity negro from the North.

Cleophus was furious. "Sir," he said, controlling his anger, "there must be a mistake in this bill."

"Make no mistake there is no mistake," said Murchison sharply. "I can count. I can add. What you see is what you get!"

"But this is a mistake," said Cleophus. "This bill is incorrect. I did not charge this amount. My bill totals only fifty-four dollars, and I have the receipts here to prove it. Your accountants have made an error."

"I have no accountants, and there is no error. I do my own accounting," said Murchison flatly.

"Yes, there is an error. I didn't charge this much in groceries! I know what I bought."

"There isn't an error. The bill is correct," said Murchison in a monotone.

"The bill ain't right!" shouted Cleophus.

"You calling me a liar in my own store, Boy? If you're calling me a liar, you had better take it back, 'cause white folks don't take too kindly to colored folks calling them a liar on their own property! Now, you had best pay your bill and get your black behind out of here 'fore something ugly happens! If you don't pay your bill, you're placing yourself in a lot of trouble."

"Who you talking about hurting, man? If anybody's gonna get a hurting up in here, it's going to be you 'cause you are all wrong, man!" said Cleophus, opening his jacket and reaching inside.

"Don't no niggers come in this store calling me no liar. Now you pay your bill or get the hell out of here," said Murchison, reaching for his black sawed-off shotgun. "I'm a member of the KKK and the citizen's council, and we don't play down here, Boy. Negroes like you come from the North looking for trouble. I'll give you trouble. I'll give you something you'll never forget! Who you think you are, anyway, with your big, black, greasy self? Who you think you are, coming in my store making trouble for me like this? I run a respectable business, and I'll be darned if a nigger like you gonna come in here questioning my authority. We does something to niggers like you down here, Boy!"

"You KKK? I'm KKKK, Ku Klux Klan Killer," said Cleophus, drawing his pearl-handled .45. "If you touch that shotgun, I'll blow your head off like you did my brother's. Except there won't be anything left of you to scrape up! Go ahead, reach! I'd love to give your employees a free holiday! Reach! You killed my brother, and I'd just love to pull the trigger on you, white boy. Just give me a reason. Just give me an excuse, and you won't ever have to worry about stocking shelves or stealing black folks' money no more. I promise you," he said, cocking the trigger with his hands trembling and swatting Murchison hard to the floor with the butt of his gun.

"Don't shoot! Don't shoot! For God's sake, don't kill me," Murchison pleaded frantically. "Please don't shoot!"

"You killed my brother, and I ought to avenge his death by killing you. You might be KKK, but I'm KKKK, except I got NYPD behind the KKKK, and that's the only thing keeping me from sending you to the cemetery like you did my brother. You remember my brother? His name was Claudell. You shot him down in cold blood 'cause he wouldn't let you cheat him no more. You cheated me like you cheated him. You shot him down like a dog and said he drew a knife on you. He never carried a knife. You killed him 'cause he wouldn't pay the bill you padded. I ought to do the same thing to you that you did to him! I ought to blow your white brains out all over this store like you did his.

"You can reach for that shotgun if you want, but you can rest assured that there will be seven walking and one talking when they carry you to the grave sight. Go ahead, make a move! I dare you to make a move! I'd love to carry your head back to New York on a platter!" shouted Cleophus.

"Please, don't kill me," Murchison pleaded, covering his head with his arms in the corner behind the counter.

"I ought to kill you right now, but what goes around comes around, and you'll be getting yours soon as the good Lord sees fit. God don't like ugly, and you and your kind been ugly towards me and mine a long, long time. It's time to put an end to people like you. It's avenging angel time. I ought to put you out of your misery, Mister, right now!" he shouted, bending down and sticking the gun into Murchison's nose. "You better be glad, but you better watch your back from now on. 'Cause every time you look around, I'll be just around the bend looking for you. Every time you move, I'm gonna be on your white behind like flies on fertilizer. Every time you even think of hurting me or mine I'm gonna be stalking you like somebody crazy. It's a shame what you did to my brother, and I ought to kill you right now! I ought to avenge all the black lives you and your kind have taken over the years—black men lynched and castrated for no reason other than looking at your ugly white women!" Then he whacked Murchison hard in the mouth with the barrel of his gun, drawing more blood. He threw fifty-four dollars in his face and turned and walked out.

Cleophus left the old man on the floor of his store, and Murchison was never the same after that. He didn't know how to handle Cleophus. He was too much of a mystery. He came then he left. From then on, Murchison was a nervous wreck, always looking over his shoulder and expecting to be sniped. He sent officers over to our home to question us about Cleophus, but we denied ever seeing him. Periodically, Cleophus would come South just to make an appearance at Murchison's store, then he'd vanish just as quickly as he came. It was a case of what goes around comes around, except full justice was not given. Claudell lost his life, but Murchison's life was spared. But it was justice in some measure because he didn't have the store much longer. The story goes that he had heart trouble. Guess all that evil he had done to black people caught up with him. He later died of a massive heart attack right there in his store. The paramedic who arrived happened to be Claudell's oldest son, Wallace. Too late. Nothing could be done. He died a slow, painful death on the floor of his store.

Throughout my life, I've seen God righting wrong and correcting situations that have gone bad. What goes around truly comes around. You reap what you sow, and sooner or later you pay for everything in this life.

I see this reality every day in people getting afflictions and illnesses mainly because of the evil and mischief they've inflicted on other folks. There's a woman who comes to me all the time for help because she can't sleep. She doesn't realize that she has insomnia probably because she's been cheating on her husband for six years. He's a good man who loves his family and takes good care of his children. But she got tired of him and sneaks around with somebody else. A lot of her illness has to do with the affair she's having with a man that doesn't even care about her. She doesn't understand that what goes around comes around. She's paying the price for having an affair that's tearing her family apart. Her husband and children don't deserve this treatment. But God has a way of straightening it all out. When the innocent suffer for no reason, those inflicting the suffering can be expected to pay up in some form or another. God will allow the pendulum of injustice to hang in the balance for just so long. Sooner or later, it's got to swing back into place.

I can say that about ninety-five percent of the people I see with various maladies and troubles are sick because of past sins and transgressions against other people. What they experience are simply the physical, psychological, and spiritual repercussions of past deeds. Not all illness can be attributed to this, but if we could trace the causes of illness, we would discover some truth to what I'm saying.

You may think this all sounds strange, but I believe God is of what goes around comes around. I told you the story about my uncle Claudell because in many respects his brother avenged his death. But there have been thousands of cases in the South where black men have been innocently lynched and their deaths have never been avenged. You can rest assured that the white folks who committed those acts may not have paid directly for their crimes, but they paid in some form or another. Perhaps they've experienced suffering in their lives which puts them in touch with the suffering they've caused others, like the death of a loved one or a close friend. The justice may not be measure for measure, but you better believe that whatever evil, injustice, or persecution they have brought on others, they have paid for it or will pay for it before their lives are over.

One of the Klan leaders saw his nine-year-old daughter suffer and die from leukemia. What goes around comes around. All the suffering he brought on black folks was returned to him by the angels of misery and suffering. Hello, pay back time.

God specializes in exacting justice in this life. Whatever we put out, we get back in some form or another. Sometimes the "comes around" takes a long time in coming around. The "goes around" may be unanswered for a long, long time. Then all of a sudden, things change and the goes around answers the comes around with lighting swiftness.

I look at all the things black folks have suffered in this country, the many injustices and troubles we've faced all along the way. God has a way of straightening things out. The movements of the 1960s were the comes around that sought to correct the goes around of the previous decades and centuries of racism and disenfranchisement. God will always find some way to set the ledgers straight. It may take a while, but it all comes back to you.

I remember a man named Clarence who was a good person. He was a perfect example of manhood in our community. Everybody loved Clarence. He always had a kind word for you and would do anything to help you out. One day they found Clarence murdered on the railroad tracks just outside of town. Some say that some white folks killed him because he had cut into the wood hauling business of some prominent businessmen in the county.

Clarence hauled wood in his horse-drawn wagon. At that time people used wood primarily to heat their stoves and homes. People—both black and white—loved Clarence so much that they bought their wood from him. He made a good living hauling wood. Some of the white folks got angry and threatened him on several occasions. He'd just smile, tip his hat, say "thank you" or "I'm sorry" and keep on going. When they found him dead, the whole town grieved. It was senseless. It was one of the biggest funerals in the history of Florida. People came from everywhere, black and white. People cried because he was such a good man.

A group of concerned black and white citizens got together to see what they could do for Clarence's family. They put out a reward for the capture of the criminals, and after several months, three eighteen-year-olds were arrested and charged with the murder. After being convicted and given fifteen years to life, the three boys were found dead in their cell blocks in prison. Rumor has it that one of the inmates ordered their execution. The inmate was James Mack White, one of the baddest negroes in the Florida penal system and the nephew of Clarence Hoskins. What goes around comes around, and you reap what you sow. Take whatever you want out of life and pay for it!

All my life I've tried to treat people right. I've tried to do the right thing. I dedicated my life to helping other people. Not because I expect something in return, but because I believe God wants me to do this. I get a measure of satisfaction helping other people, especially when they can't help themselves.

I believe God ultimately cares about all of us. That's why God wants to make sure that everyone is given his due and everyone pays according to what he takes out of life. We can't expect to go through life without some form of retribution for the decisions and choices we've made. God couldn't handle the world without having what goes around come around.

In every aspect of life we see this. In nature, all the natural disasters, the hurricanes, tornadoes, and earthquakes are God's way of correcting the abuse man has done to the environment. I'm not saying everything is due to abuse, but sicknesses we have today and the problems with our health are related to the way we have mishandled nature. The water is poisoned. The air is polluted. We must pay a price for having wreaked so much havoc on mother nature.

In politics, business, and every aspect of life, we see the pendulum swinging. There was a time when Japanese products were a joke to Americans. Not anymore. What goes around comes around. Communist governments enslaved their people. Now the walls of communism have tumbled down, and it's a new day.

"What goes around comes around" is God's way of wiping clean the blood-stained slate of humankind. It is God's way of telling the innocent that he is on their side. God always finds a way of correcting each human situation. Without God's best efforts in this regard, humankind would be more hopeless and despondent than ever. It is because people believe that God will correct all wrong that they can live with the hope of a better day tomorrow. Whatever our problems and concerns are, God will straighten them all out in his own time and in his own way. We just have to keep believing that with all our minds, hearts, and souls.

Black people in America must believe that whatever injustices and hardships have been placed upon them will be one day completely abolished, because God will bring in a new and glorious Day. The lives of the Clarence Hoskinses and Claudell Pettifords will have new meaning in the hallowed halls of justice in the sacred courts of God's universe, because he is God of what goes around comes around. Believing this helps us to live each day with a quiet expectation that however bad things become, God will sooner or later straighten it all out to the benefit of his beloved people.

Commentary

Indigenous black theology affirms the God of racial and human justice. This principle of justice, either actualized or anticipated, is an integral facet of black life in America. Whatever injustices have been experienced will one day he compensated.

Having seen her share of racial inhumanity in the South, Beulah is acutely aware of the perils of life in America. She understands that one of the sustaining hopes of African American people is the belief that God is ultimately in charge of the universe and that no one ever escapes the judgment of sins committed against the innocent. God cannot stand to see his children suffer and thus always finds a way to make wrong right. The great crucible of American society is the problem of race. It is under this banner that America's most atrocious crimes have been committed and the most injustice experienced. Accordingly, God will find a way to compensate black people for all the crimes and persecutions they have suffered. The suffering inflicted by whites on blacks may not, however, be the same suffering they themselves experience. Retribution may come in other forms which are just as afflicting and painful as those experienced by blacks. White people may not suffer from racial discrimination and persecution, but their payment will be made in forms equally devastating. There is no way that God will discount all the evil of whites against blacks without making them pay for their crimes.

This truth is not only applicable to white/black relations but to black/black relations and human relations in general. Whatever the form, color, or shape of injustice, those committing the injustice must pay in some form or another. This view differs from the Christian doctrine of forgiveness and atonement which is preceded by confession. Because the evil of racial discrimination and persecution has been so thoroughly and intentionally sustained for so long, atonement and redemption cannot apply. It is only through God's exacting, punitive judgment that any true compensation may be obtained, especially when racism has become less an error of individual ignorance and omission and more an institutional practice in American society. Some crimes and sins have been so advertently and intentionally practiced over the long haul that they do not qualify as forgivable sins. They are as determinately executed as a tennis pro practicing his back hand. They are deliberate, forceful, and systemic. The only way God can redeem such situations is by having what goes around come around. The great day of reckoning for the crimes of race has not yet been experienced by those responsible for sustaining this evil.

As stated earlier, this God of justice shows his presence not only in areas of race matters but in all human situations where evil and inhumanity have been inflicted on the innocent. Black people committing crimes against each other will have their day in court. The issue therefore is not simply a matter of race but a matter of humanity. How long will the innocent be required to suffer at the hands of those who make a living at preying on them? Some acts are beyond the veil of forgiveness and redemption, and thus some other form of retribution is necessary to eradicate the injustice. Everybody must pay sooner or later. If you don't pay now, you must pay later.

This notion of God has universal implications. None of us escapes the imprint of the consequences our actions have on those around us. Everything we do in life makes its mark, leaves its stain, or impresses itself on the outer world. We must be held accountable for all that we do. The idea of God forgiving and erasing those mistakes we intentionally and repeatedly commit against others must be reversed through some windfall or painstaking reparation process.

Indigenous black theology affirms the primacy and value of such a viewpoint. The God of truth and justice will forever find ways of eliminating injustice and untruth. This is the driving force of nature and the compelling impetus of humanity's striving for freedom, justice, and equality. Because God will ultimately correct that which is wrong and hold accountable those who have committed evil against the innocent, the hope of humankind is that we all will see this justice come to fruition and reality in our own lives.

Conclusion

When I submitted this manuscript to several publishers, some reviewers wondered if "indigenous" would be an appropriate term to describe black theology. One writer argued that the term was antiquated and should be discarded altogether, while another indicated that such a concept best describes native theology or the theology of first peoples rather than black theology. But I believe that while the term "indigenous" may connote the theologies and cultures of natives peoples, it's also relevant to the African American cultural experience. "Indigenous" for my purposes means "from the ground up," or that which derives its purpose, focus, and understanding from the lived lexicons and cultural archives of the African American experience. These experiences are indigenous in that they are native to a particular context. They are part of a theological vernacular which is emblematic of black life in America.

This means that black theology is precisely indigenous insofar as it primarily emanates from the uniquely lived cultural ethos of African Americans and not primarily from the written texts of academia or Euro-American culture. Since a distinguishing characteristic of the African American experience is the sharing of knowledge, information concepts, and ideas though the oral narrative rather than through written analytical transmissions, indigenous black theology fashions itself in accordance with these specific cultural norms. This does not mean that indigenous black theology does not draw from written sources. It only means that those sources emanate from within the context of African American life.

Thus, much of what is formulated and understood about God from the indigenous black viewpoint issues principally from the oral transmission of knowledge and the lived narrative experiences of God in day-to-day black life. The indigenous character of black theology lies precisely in its ability to develop understandings of God without relying upon the writings of other theologians, sacred texts, or other written forms of knowledge and information so essential in the formation of traditional academic theology. Some indigenous black theology may draw upon various and sundry written texts, both within and outside of black culture. But these are not the primary modes of sharing or recording understandings of God.

This is not a devaluation of traditional or academic theology or the sacred texts of established religions. It only means that black indigenous theology does not develop solely through the use of these primary source data. Indigenous black theology employs the use of different sources as the basis for developing understandings of God. These sources include the folkways, mores, and extant cultural realities and truths of the African American experience as well as the sacred texts of established religions.

The preceding narratives, then, according to the indigenous viewpoint, are not so much definitions as they are descriptions of the indigenous realities of God. They depict interpretations of God based on lived experiences and do not attempt to define the reality of God in any Western academic sense. The idea of the "reality" of God is utilized instead of the "concept" of God, because it suggests a much broader interpretive and experiential framework for understanding God's revelation in the context of lived personal experiences.

In street corner or indigenous black theology, descriptions of God experiences become windows and metaphors for unearthing deeper realities of God. Since the reality of God is lived each day, new depictions and understandings of God largely emanate from the multiplexed configuration of the black experience and are transmitted primarily through both the written and oral archives of black culture.

The narratives in this book attempt to describe the reality of God from the indigenous black viewpoint, which draws the heart of theological development from the raw lived experiences of African American life and culture. These reflections provide a glimpse into what some black people think about God and illustrate the fact that what they think and how they came to their ideas seldom fit within the established norms of academic theology. And although these descriptions of the reality of God do not fit within the hermeneutical norms of academic theology, it is important to remember that these perspectives are no less legitimate.

The fact that these "God realities" emerge from both the written and oral archives of black culture suggests that the archives themselves function as a self-corroborating authority. Black life and culture are shaped by certain norms and realities which both establish and reinforce the authenticity of black life and experience. The truth of black existence is established through the lived experience of black life and culture. According to the indigenous viewpoint, what I think about God and how I arrive at that understanding will be confirmed within the boundaries of truth established within the culture of my own experience. Thus, for example, Winston's observation that Charlie Parker is the ultimate manifestation of the creativity of God in human form is a truth established within the norms of his cultural experience as a black person in America. It doesn't matter that this theological observation seems frivolous to professional or traditional theologians. Winston has arrived at his own truth about God within the realm of his own cultural reality. Nor does it matter that for some people, white as well as black, Charlie Parker was a jazz musician who died from a drug overdose.

For such people, equating Charlie Parker's genius with the creativity of God is sacrilegious. The seemingly undisciplined life and bad habits which led to Parker's demise are inimical to the disciplined life of the spiritual visionary. Nothing could be farther from established theological truths than affirming Charlie Parker as a manifestation of God's creative genius. In fact, some would argue that because it *seemed* that Parker led a godless life, God couldn't possibly have anything to do with his musical genius.

But for Winston and others like him, Parker's genius was a manifestation of the creativity of God reaching previously unrealized heights. His drug overdose does not obscure the sanctity of his spiritual presence or the meaning and vitality he brought to thousands of lives. The medium just happened to be black music, but it could just have easily been science, industry, or even religion itself. But the reality of God from Winston's black indigenous viewpoint does not have to be ostensibly religious or spiritual to have theological value and import. The fact that Charlie Parker was a jazz musician makes his position as a manifestation of God's creativity no less plausible than if he were a classical or folk musician. For Winston, Charlie Parker embodied an epiphany of creative ideas, which for him was a Pentecostal spiritual experience. Hearing Parker play opened corridors in his being and soul and gave him glimpses of the eternal in ways that traditional church hymns and established music couldn't. So do we say, then, that Winston's experience is not authentically theological, that what he experienced in hearing the Yard Bird play was something less than religious?

Both Anglo culture and academe might repudiate such claims because they do not conform to the canons of existing theological truths. But the ethos shaping Winston's perspective is authentic to the forms and norms of African American culture and is therefore a legitimate context for the realization of God.

The same is true for Hakeem, Julia, and the others. Their understanding of who God is and how God works grows out of personal experience. This experience, the foundation of which is black life and culture, has its own narrative realities and truths, its own body of information and knowledge, and its own corroborative and valuating authorities which shape understandings of God. They influence God's work in their lives. Such understandings are not mediated through the writings of other theologians, the Bible, or other sacred texts but rather through the archives of black culture which establish and corroborate their own value and truth in accordance with the realities of black life in America.

Hakeem's assertion that God encourages him to protect his sacred self by carrying the AK47 is a truth rising out of his own daily experiences in the streets of Detroit. Again, the bodies of knowledge and information that establish sacred truths are not always found in the sacred texts of organized religion, in canons of previously established religious beliefs, or in the hallowed halls of university consortiums. Instead, they are found in the lived archives and lexicons of the black cultural experience. For example, the cultural truths prompting Christians to staunchly uphold non-violence as a means of protecting and ensuring the sanctity of life may be different from the cultural truths compelling Hakeem to carry a weapon to protect himself from violence.

The religious and spiritual truths of personal lived experiences therefore may depart in form and substance from previously established theological truths. Lived experience establishes its own archives of knowledge and truth, which do not always conform to the norms or the conventional thought of the larger culture. The value and sanctity of these truths lie in the fact that they are different and provide avenues of meaning to the human search for God. What Hakeem believes about God is truth for him because it allows him to survive on the streets of the big city. His belief brings value, sanctity, and purpose to a life that might otherwise be lost in the chaos of a precarious existence.

Julia's experience with incest helped establish her understanding of God. In coming to terms with the truth of her experience, she developed a concept of God which allowed her to transcend potential barriers. Part of the contention of indigenous theology is that there is a single experience or series of personal lived experiences which have more impact in shaping understandings of God than anything else. These experiences are the dynamic formative influences on theological development and do not always conform to the normative trajectory of theological experiences. In addition, from these experiences arises a fundamental truth about the reality of God which, if pushed, can be a springboard for further theological exploration.

Each narrative in this book has disclosed a fundamental truth about its author's understanding of God. When explored fully and analyzed, this truth reveals something about the person's quest for personal meaning and wholeness. It establishes its own archive, which serves as a metaphor for the dissemination and discovery of additional meaningful truths about God and life itself. For example, Larry's digital theology is a metaphor for the importance of spiritual concentration in finding a path to God and the deeper human quest for personal meaning and fulfillment. Although he is homosexual and dying of AIDS, the digital machines become his metaphor for the mastery of other truths and realities. His concentration on the digital readouts allows him to transcend time and space, to become something other than a person dying of AIDS.

The truth of human concentration becomes a metaphor for truth in the discovery of God. The believer cannot find God without some measure of disciplined concentration, be it through prayer, fasting, or some other spiritual activity.

I don't mean to oversimplify here, but each narrator's understanding of God sheds light on an enduring truth about the reality of God in the African American experience. This particular truth discloses something about the nature of indigenous black theology and the versatile nature of African American life and culture. Whether it's Charlie Parker being seen as a manifestation of the creative mind of God or Hakeem's assertion that carrying the AK47 is an act of the sacred, the archives of truth giving rise to these theological perspectives are deeply rooted in African American culture. The culture develops its

138

own truths and sets its own standards and rules for human existence. Indigenous black theology affirms both the narrative form in which these truths are conveyed and the black cultural context that constitutes the foundation of all lived personal indigenous God encounters.

What I have sought to do in these narratives is provide a glimpse into indigenous perspectives of God, which are quite different from conventional theological interpretation. While academic theology has done much to broaden our understanding of God, it has not gone far enough in exploring the perspectives of indigenous grass roots people. Furthermore, while black liberation theology has given us a rich interpretation of the legacy of freedom inherent in black life, it has not delineated the other truths of black life which make it a seedbed of spiritual creativity. Thus, indigenous black theology is theology whose fundamental truths and sources are derived from the canons, archives, and lexicons of all African American cultural experiences. It is theology which embraces the full complement of lived black experience in America.

Some would argue that my commentaries as postscript analyses are simply too academic. In response, I would argue that my purpose here is to explicate indigenous thought in conventional theological terms. Because this theology does not emerge from academia does not mean it cannot share common ground with it. I would furthermore argue that I am not negating the value of intellectual analysis in conveying ideas. I am only affirming that the university and academia are not the primary sources of indigenous black theology, nor do they provide the foundational interpretive framework for delineating black indigenous people's understandings of God, especially those which emerge from the streeets.

My hope is that these narratives will precipitate dialogue about the ways people cultivate their particular theologies and that this dialogue will take place between street theologians and academic theologians. While each has much in common with the other, they can both learn much from each other in ways which will help us all better understand the reality of God wherever we exist.

139